How To Talk To

Overcome shyness, social anxiety and low self-confidence & be able to chat to anyone!

Dr. Jennifer Alison

Copyright © Jennifer Alison Publishing

All rights reserved.
No part of this publication may be reproduced, distributed, or transmitted in any form or by any means, including photocopying, recording, or other electronic or mechanical methods, without the prior written permission of the publisher, except in the case of brief quotations embodied in critical reviews and certain other non-commercial uses permitted by copyright law.

About The Author

Dr. Jennifer Alison received her doctoral degree from Illinois School of Professional Psychology in Chicago and her Masters degree in Applied Psychology from the University of Baltimore.

Dr Alison specializes in the treatment of anxiety disorders and related physiological issues and has published several papers and books on this subject as well as speaking at conferences around the world.

Jennifer Alison divides her time between New York and London with her husband Stephen.

facebook.com/drjenniferalison

Table of Contents

Introduction: Quickly Learn How To Talk To Anyone

Part One: Overcoming Conversational Obstacles Fast
Conversation In The Digital Age
Conversation & Quickly Overcoming Your Personal Limits
What Is Holding You Back & How To Overcome It

Part Two: Learn How To Talk To Anyone!
Become The Conversationalist You Always Wanted To Be
The Secret Trick That Makes Conversation So Much Better!
Breaking Bad Habits Forever
Overcoming Difficult Thoughts & Feelings
10 Things People Want From A Conversation

Part Three: Simple Techniques To Improve Your Conversational Prowess
The Successful Conversationalist
Top 15 Skills For The Great Conversationalist
Dealing With Specific Circumstances
Progress With Life, Do Not Let The Fear Hold You Back

Introduction – Quickly Learn How To Talk To Anyone

Conversation and communication are not easy. They are integral parts of life but can be more complicated than one might think. These skills don't come easily to everyone. There are approximately 15 million people in the United States suffering from social anxiety and a further 6 million who experience panic attacks. If you suffer from anxiety disorders or low self-esteem, talking to people can be nerve wracking. **But it's not just people with anxiety disorders that feel uncomfortable conversing!**

There are countless individuals who simply find communication difficult regardless of their emotional stability. They might avoid social outings due to anxiety or clam up during conversations. They may have difficulties being assertive or facing conflict. Whether you've been asked to do a speech at a friend's wedding, you've been set up on a blind date, or you have to talk to your boss about some changes in work, if conversation doesn't come naturally to you, you might be overcome with nervousness and find yourself saying things that you later regret or worry about. The fact is, not everyone on earth finds conversation easy. Many of us need to actively learn conversational skills in order to become comfortable and confident communicators.

There are a wide variety of reasons you might find conversation anxiety provoking. One of the most prominent causes of the recent rise in social anxiety and conversational awkwardness is the undeniable fact that certain changes in technology have completely rewritten how we communicate with one another.

 Before there was texting and emailing, people used to talk on the phone far more than we do now. They would catch up with friends and family over coffee and generally spend more time in the company of others. But as time goes on, we are becoming more and more used to hiding behind screens, making the idea of sitting face-to-face with someone feel almost alien. Texting, emailing, and social media forums forms a physical boundary between us and the person we are speaking to as well as giving us a chance to think before we reply.

You might write twenty-five drafts of an email before sending it or wait to respond to a text until you've given it plenty of thought. Unfortunately, face-to-face and telephone conversations put us in a position where we are forced to think *fast*. We can prepare for conversations to some extent but we never know exactly how a conversation is going to go until we're actually in it. When we're communicating in person, our conversational partners can see the subtle changes in our facial expressions and body language. They might misread our movements or misunderstand us if our facial expressions contradict the message we're trying to portray. They may challenge or disagree with the things we say leaving us feeling even more nervous and uncomfortable.

Many of us are unaware or unsure of what our body is communicating while we navigate conversations. Often body language alone can cause your views to be misinterpreted without you even knowing it. What's worse is the underlying fear of saying something stupid and ending up feeling embarrassed or ashamed. You might have a generalized fear that you won't be able to get your point across exactly the way that you'd like. Your mind might race during conversations, making it hard to concentrate and filling your head with unhelpful thoughts. *What if I make a fool of myself? What if other people notice how uncomfortable I am? What if they laugh at me or judge me? What happens if there's an awkward silence?*

This book begins with a brief section discussing the many possible reasons people might find conversing with others difficult. It will explore things like personality types, past experience, and other obstacles, giving you an opportunity to think about what factors in your life may have informed the way you feel about conversation. Taking the opportunity to learn more about yourself will help you to better understand your instincts, fears, and potential mishaps when it comes to communication.

Throughout the rest of the book I will take you through an in-depth look at the act of conversation, so that you can quickly become a better, more confident conversationalist. I will focus on what people really want from a conversation, so as to give you a deeper understanding of others and how to keep your conversations polite, productive, and enjoyable. You will be encouraged to think about how conversation features in your life so that you can identify your personal difficulties and conquer them. I will also highlight some common negative thoughts and habits that could be causing you added stress, as well as looking into some ways you might better cope with difficult situations. I will equip you with the practical skills you need to make your conversations easy and stress free.

Finally I will discuss a number of specific situations where communication skills are vital. These will include everyday circumstances with friends and family members, coping with social anxiety at work, getting comfortable with social gatherings and dating, job interviews, speaking to a group, dealing with conflict, and more.

Life is so much better when you have the ability to talk to anyone without fear. Do not let the dread hold you back anymore. Life is too short. My aim is to give you the confidence you need to overcome conversational awkwardness.

Let's get started…

Part One: Overcoming Conversational Obstacles Fast

The first part of this book will supply you with some basic information about conversation and why some of us find it so hard. Here I will discuss how changes in the world around us may be causing increased social ineptness and how you can overcome it. I will encourage you to think about your own personal limits where communication is concerned, by talking you through a number of personality traits and experiences that may have contributed to the way you talk to people. These will include things like low self-esteem, difficult past experiences, and limited social practice to name just a few.

This section is an important part of your journey towards conversational confidence and as such, I encourage you to resist skipping it. Understanding yourself, your instincts, feelings, and behavior is an integral part of self-growth. This book is designed not only to give you the skills you need to become a better conversationalist, but also to encourage you to think more deeply about your experiences with other people. This way, you will not merely soak up a host of generic advice, but rather, you will actually change the way you think about social situations, thus achieving a more powerful, lasting change.

Conversation in the Digital Age

It's important to note that conversation and communication are hard for everyone at one point or another. It is not a difficulty that only strikes people who are under confident, nor is it something that only people with anxiety disorders experience. Even the most confident extroverts can experience anxiety and worry when it comes to communication. In fact, even people whom you perceive to be cool, calm, and collected will struggle when talking to people from time to time. This is an obstacle that most of us face at different times in our lives and I encourage you to remind yourself of that fact anytime you find yourself feeling low over things like this. When it comes to self-improvement, it pays to be kind to yourself rather than falling into habits of putting yourself down.

One major problem we face in the world today is that *so* much of our communication relies on the written word. As I mentioned earlier, email, social media and texting have begun to take the place of face-to-face meetings and telephone calls. But no matter how much our lives change with new technology and the ever quickening pace of life, we still have to talk to other people now and again. The fact is, although it may seem easier to communicate in the aforementioned ways, these changes in society could very likely be *increasing* your conversational anxiety.

These days almost all of us are getting used to having brief, de-humanized "conversations" with people via computers, tablets, and mobile phones. And although these devices can be wonderful when we need a quick answer or other brief exchange, many people these days are relying on them completely, rarely ever actually *speaking* to anyone anymore. Thus, we are becoming impersonal in a way; replacing most, if not all of our communication with electronic devices and reducing what *would be* conversations down to a few short lines. This is almost always because it can be much easier to compose a text or message online; so much less stressful, less time consuming, less nerve wracking. But if this is the case in your life and you really want to improve your social skills, it would be wise to consider making some changes so that you can let go of this crutch and get some real life conversational practice.

The astounding change in the way we communicate happened fast and it has become a factor in nearly all of our lives. You might be wondering what it is about these new ways of communication that's so bad. You might be thinking that actually, you find emails and texts a lot easier than having proper conversations with people. But that's exactly my point. There is a certain feeling of safety and comfort in knowing that we don't have to face our conversational partners. It takes a lot of pressure off us, especially if we struggle with social anxiety or awkwardness. This way of communicating creates a boundary between us and the rest of the world. Our mobile phones keep us removed from other people and our computers create a barrier that helps us feel safe and secure.

You might feel like it's easier to be your true self online. You might really enjoy the freedom you have to present yourself they way you'd like to be perceived; to hide your weaknesses or even be anonymous. These are all natural feelings and in essence, there is nothing wrong with any of these ideas. However, allowing yourself to rely on your electronic devices for all or most of your communication with other people can backfire. Not only can the tone of what you're saying get lost in the mix (causing you to be misunderstood or worse), but the more you maintain that barrier between yourself and other people, the harder it will be to converse face to face.

For example think about a time you had to call in sick from work. You had to speak to your boss and explain why you wouldn't be able to make it in. Even if you were genuinely ill, you may have felt anxious or nervous. Perhaps you worried that your boss wouldn't believe you, maybe you'd had a period of multiple absences that had caused some tension in the workplace. Making that call and having to meet face-to-face with your boss again later may have filled you with dread. You may have found it so stressful that you didn't end up making the phone call at all and ended up in a worse position afterward. If you had been allowed or able to text or email rather than speak directly to your boss, how much easier would you have found that situation? Would you have found writing a text or email nerve wracking at all? Perhaps.

But would you have felt the same degree of nervousness? It's doubtful. I brought this example up because it seems pretty obvious - pretty logical - that most of us would prefer the option to face something difficult while hiding behind a boundary. In a way, it's like having a shield in a battle. It might make you feel more confident, less afraid, stronger, less likely to be harmed or misunderstood, etc. But the thing is, the less we converse with other people and the more we rely on communication behind a shield, the less able we will be when it comes to having true conversations.

Think of conversation as a "use it or lose it" skill. Talking to people takes practice and the more you avoid it, the harder it becomes.

You may have noticed that nowadays that it's not only difficult situations that we chose to "hide" from. In fact, the vast majority of our communication with others may be occurring behind that same boundary. Even something as simple and easy as sending a birthday wish to a friend is now more likely to happen online than by any other means. Many of us seek the easiest, fastest, and most guarded ways to talk to other people at all costs. Communicating in this manner, hiding behind texts or online messages, has a way of keeping your conversational partners in the dark to some extent. They can't see your body language or read your facial expressions. You can present yourself in a far more calculated way, showing the parts of yourself that you're comfortable with and hiding the qualities you dislike. You can think before you "speak". You can say what you think people want to hear rather than accidentally blurting out your true feelings. It's almost as if your conversational partner is more of an *opponent* and you don't want them to see you sweat.

The problem with all of this is *not* that "talking" via the written word is entirely negative, awful or dangerous. It's more about how using these skills and devices gives us fewer opportunities to have face to face conversations; thus making talking to people more and more difficult as time goes on. The more "social" we are online, the less social we are becoming in the real world. Conversation takes practice for most people; it's a skill that needs refining. The more we talk to other people, the easier it gets, the more confident we feel, and the more successful our communication is.

Imagine a person who goes to a spin class every day. They spend an hour each morning riding a stationary bike and it makes them feel great. But imagine that same person can't actually ride a real bike. They've never gone out and cycled with the wind in their face watching the world whiz by. Now imagine this person spontaneously decides that they'd like to take their strong and confident spin muscles out on the road. What is likely to happen? They might get on a real bike and feel extremely unstable, shaky, and imbalanced. They might not be able to ride the real bike at all, leaving them with two options: learn how to ride a real bike or go back to the gym and forget that real bikes exist at all.

Now, regardless of how you feel about bikes or gyms, think about this example in the context of conversation. You might feel great online. You get to be funny and entertaining without leaving your own living room. You get to offer congratulations and condolences to your friends without even getting dressed. You can send birthday wishes to an acquaintance over social media in less than a minute and then get on with your day. You might feel more calm and confident when faced with conflict. You might feel safer knowing that you can reply to emails on your own time or simply switch your phone off when things get awkward or difficult. But what happens when you get back in the real world and sit face to face with another person?

Can you use your online skills when it comes to actually speaking to someone in person?
Do the same congratulations and condolences translate to the spoken word?
What about the ability to control your facial expressions and your body language?
And what if you say something wrong or you become misunderstood?

How will you navigate a situation if you say something less-than-smart or if you offend someone accidentally?
How will you feel if your conversational partner says something that you find to be rude?
What will you do? How will you cope with silence? How will you cope with conflict?

When sitting face to face with someone, you won't be able to close your laptop and think about it over a quiet cup of tea. You won't be able to switch your phone off, assess the situation, and return to the conversation later with a brief apology about having been away from your phone. This is exactly what I mean when I say that communicating behind computers and mobile phones can make conversations harder for you in the long run.

If you are the type of person who often replaces real life conversations with texts or emails, it's time to set those vices aside. Start practicing talking to people over the next week. Challenge yourself to have as many verbal conversations as possible. Think of this as stretching your conversational muscles. Rather than typing up a short response to a friend, pick up the phone and call them.

Schedule a coffee date with someone you feel comfortable with or visit some family members throughout the week. As you converse with people, take note of any things you find difficult.

Are there certain topics that make you clam up?
Do you feel uncomfortable when people give you attention or praise?
Do you often say (or *think* you say) the wrong thing or misunderstand people?
Do others misunderstand you?

After you have a conversation with someone, ask yourself if it was a success and think about why it was or wasn't. Think about what topics you found easy and which you found challenging. Think about which people you felt the most comfortable talking to and why. In addition to this, take some time to evaluate how much you rely on electronic devices and try to think about why this is.

Are there certain conversations that are easier to have when you're not face to face with someone? If so, is that because the topic is simple and relatively unimportant or is it because the topic is quite serious and talking in person would be difficult and/or anxiety provoking?

Taking the time to get to know yourself better and reflect in this manner is a great way to get a handle on what your personal obstacles are. It may seem silly to have "practice conversations" but the more you do things like this, the easier it will be to become the conversationalist you'd like to be. Remember all skills take practice and getting to know yourself better is something everyone can benefit from.

Conversation & Quickly Overcoming Your Personal Limits

When it comes to struggling with conversations, texts and emails are by no means the only factors that could be making things difficult for you. Unfortunately, people struggled with conversation long before those things even existed. Think of some of your favorite books and movies. How many times have you seen a character get nervous when faced with difficult social situations? How many scenes have included someone feeling nervous and awkward around their boss, their father-in-law, and the person they're in love with? Far too many to count! Conflict and conversational anxiety are some of the most common plot devices used in literature and film because nearly *all* of us can relate to those struggles. Every one of us will experience these things time and time again throughout our lives; however, this does not mean that all of your conversations need to be awkward and uncomfortable.

If you want to become a great conversationalist, taking the time to explore some events in your life that may have held you back in the first place could be of great benefit. Asking yourself questions and reflecting on how you got where you are today can have a massive impact on what your life will be like tomorrow.

What is it that makes it hard for you to talk to people?
What obstacles do you face as an individual that are impacting the way you feel and behave around other people?
How do you feel when facing conflict and why?
Do you struggle with feelings of inferiority?
Are you afraid of rejection and ridicule?
Are you holding onto past embarrassments?
Do you find it difficult to start conversations or to keep them going?
Can you identify any early experiences that may have contributed to how you feel when talking to people?

Understanding why we struggle with certain things in life is the first step towards overcoming them. The following list briefly outlines some feelings, personality traits, and experiences that may have contributed to the anxiety you experience when talking to people.

Things That Could Be Holding You Back & How To Overcome Them

Low Self Esteem
Living with low self-esteem can cause problems in almost every aspect of your life but it can be particularly harmful when it comes to talking to people. Unfortunately, when it comes to matters relating to maintaining healthy relationships with friends and family and climbing the career ladder, having both low self-esteem *and* difficulty expressing yourself can be a toxic cocktail. If you have particularly low feelings of self-worth or patterns of self-loathing and self-ridicule, it's no surprise that you might find talking to people a bit unnerving at times.

Being low in confidence or believing yourself to be *"weird"*, *"different"*, or *"not good enough"* could make you feel like the black sheep in social situations. You might be afraid of standing out too much or feel like you'd rather blend into the scenery and become invisible than having any attention on you. You might be completely floored by a conversation that has turned negative or you may become devastated by a relationship that has gone sour due to your poor communication skills.

People with low self-esteem often struggle with social anxiety but in addition to that, they may also struggle to recognize when they've experienced *healthy* and *positive* communication with another person. Instead, they may develop habits of focusing on their shortcomings, indulging in pessimistic projections, and feeding their poor self-beliefs with habitual negative mantras. It's common for people with low self-esteem to find conflict and negativity completely disarming. They may worry excessively about how a conversation or social situation will end up; thus increasing their anxiety and decreasing their confidence. Later, they may think back on conversations and other situations and put themselves down for even the slightest social mishap.

A common misconception about people with low self-esteem is that they are all shy and quiet. But this belief is entirely untrue. Every person with low self-esteem is different. Everyones self esteem has been formed by their own individual life experiences. The relationships you've had, the conflicts you've faced, and the traumatic or devastating memories you possess, all inform how you feel about yourself. Similarly, low self-esteem affects everyone's lives in different ways. Many people living with low self-esteem are actually quite good at hiding it; in fact, they might not even know that their self-esteem is low. Those who bully or ridicule others are equally likely to have self-esteem as those who are passive or lacking in confidence. Many people will fail to recognize how their poor self-beliefs affect their every day life.

Self-esteem is a complex part of human life. It can present in many different ways for many different reasons. Often the people who are the loudest - those who brag about themselves and/or blame others for their own shortcomings - behave the way they do as a result of low self-esteem and/or insecurity. People like this may come across as rude or arrogant to other people. They may be socially inept, highly critical of other people, or exceedingly withholding of their own true thoughts and feelings. They might come across as guarded or suspicious. Other people with low self-esteem are quiet, reserved, fearful of conflict and confrontation, less likely to put themselves ahead of others and unable to think highly of themselves. You can imagine how feelings like these might hold someone back from being able to talk to other people with ease. If you are preoccupied with negative views of yourself - whether those views are inferior or superior to others - it's likely that asserting yourself confidently and appropriately will be difficult.

Recovering from low self-esteem is entirely possible. It takes time and patience but overcoming it can completely change how you view yourself and the world around you. It is a journey worth embarking on. But for now, the good news is that when it comes to talking to people, low self-esteem does not have to be a major obstacle.

Throughout this book, you will develop the skills and knowledge you need to talk to anyone regardless of your private self-beliefs. What's even better is that as you perfect the art of conversation, your self-esteem will naturally benefit. Learning new skills and taking steps to improve yourself and your life is a fantastic way to start changing any negative feelings you may have of yourself.

A Difficult Past
If your childhood, adolescence, and/or early adulthood were particularly difficult, you may have been prevented from developing the social skills one needs to comfortably talk to other people. If you were abused in any way at any age, your feelings about other people could be dramatically different from those people who didn't experience such things. You may be wary of other people, suspicious, jumpy, fearful, or entirely lacking in confidence. If you have been through trauma or any type of emotional instability, it is possible and common to feel as though you are set apart or "different" from other people. You may struggle to hold yourself in the same esteem in which you hold other people. You may undervalue yourself, feel inadequate, put other people on pedestals, or simply feel uncomfortable talking to people. Furthermore, having a difficult past may have meant that you experienced a lack of emotional support and/or encouragement when it came to personal growth. Living with an abusive, absent, or neglectful parent could have been a huge obstacle in your life. So too, being overlooked, ignored, or regularly compared to a more "successful" sibling or friend could continue to haunt you in adulthood.

There are many things that could've made your past difficult and not all of them involve extreme or dramatic events. For instance, if there is anything about you that set you apart from others such as having a disability, coming from a low income household, or receiving inadequate education, living with that difference may have shaped how you view yourself within the world around you. It may have made talking to people daunting and anxiety provoking.

Imagine a person who is disabled or someone who has a learning difficulty and think about the ways they may be treated that could make them think of their *difference* as more of a *flaw*. Imagine a young person who doesn't fit into gender norms; a young boy who likes ballet instead of football or a girl who would rather build things with her dad and brothers than have giggly sleepovers with her friends. Think about the ways these young people may have struggled to fit in, to be taken seriously, to express themselves honestly and be accepted among their peers.

Take some time to think about your upbringing and your childhood in general. Can you identify any events in your past that might have made you feel under confident when it comes to talking to people? Ask yourself the following questions to help you along.

Was there a time you felt more comfortable communicating with others? If so, what happened that might have affected that?
What made you stand out when you were young? Is there something that makes you stand out now?
Were you often faced with rejection?
Did you feel valued and respected as a young person? Do you now?
How did you cope with difficult times in your past?
Were you encouraged to talk about your feelings or keep your cards close to you chest?

When someone is regularly put down or ridiculed, they are likely developing negative feelings about themselves and the people around them to some degree. Similarly, if someone is put under unreasonable amounts of pressure at a young age, or if they cease to live up to unreasonably high standards, they may automatically develop poor self-beliefs. If that person is then encouraged to hide their feelings rather than exploring and expressing them, they may grow up believing that their feelings are signs of weakness. If you were encouraged to keep people at arm's length, you might feel uncomfortable or suspicious when people show a genuine interest in you. Furthermore, if you were abused and/or mistreated in your past, you may have developed exceedingly negative beliefs about yourself. You may have a hard time accepting compliments or letting people get close to you. You may struggle to recognize any positive traits that you possess.

If you are scared - on some level - that your negative experiences will repeat themselves, holding yourself back from talking to people might actually be an ineffective attempt at protecting yourself. As we progress through life, it's extremely important that we have people in our lives that we can trust. We need to be able to be our true selves and to be heard without fear of ridicule or rejection. In order to be able to live fully in the present, it's important to do what you can to recover from painful events in your past.

Overcoming an abusive or traumatic past isn't always easy but it is possible. Trying to move beyond your past can dramatically change the shape of your future. Learning to talk to people is a great way to begin a more positive, confident future for yourself. The more conversational skills you develop, the better you'll feel about yourself. And the better you feel about yourself, the easier talking to people will be. Take time to reflect on some of your past experiences and think about if and how they function in your life today. Ask yourself if those experiences are serving you positively or if they're holding you back. If your past experiences are keeping you from enjoying your present day life, try to allow yourself to let them go. These experiences are not who you are, they are merely places you've been. Imagine yourself being released from the negative events tying you to your difficult past. Visualize yourself the way you want to be now and in the future and remind yourself regularly that you *can* have those things. You deserve to live the life you want. Your past does not have to dictate your future.

A Need For Approval
Although this is often something we try to hide in life, having a need for approval is an extremely natural part of human existence. As children, most of us gained this fundamental need in school and at home. Our teachers praised us when we got good grades or helped out our classmates. Our parents recognized our achievements with appropriate acknowledgement and rewards. Our friends may have held us in high esteem for accomplishments in team sports or other group activities. Even in adulthood most of us desire and seek approval to some extent. We work to the best of our ability so as to

earn promotions and increased pay. We present ourselves in ways that we hope others will respect.

However, if your life lacked approval and appreciation growing up, it is entirely natural that your need for approval as an adult might be a little bit stronger than most. This is not uncommon and it need not be a permanent fixture in your life. Your desire for approval does not mean that you are weak or needy, but it can make communication difficult at times. Often, if someone has a particularly strong need for approval, their conversational manner will show this to some extent. Everyone is different and for that reason our behavior can range dramatically. For instance, having a deep need for approval could mean that you shut down and begin feeling shame or self-loathing when others have achieved more than you. It might make you unreasonably defensive at times. You may develop habits of working too hard or having an intense focus on the idea of success.

Similarly, you might find yourself to be overly critical when other people accomplish things, thus making people think of you as rude or arrogant. On the other end of the spectrum, your need for approval might make you exceedingly quiet or shy. You might be nervous or uncomfortable when you've accomplished something genuinely worthy of praise and approval. Most people in this category will struggle with insecurity in different ways throughout their lives.

Overcoming a strong need for approval is entirely possible but it requires regular self-reflection. The most powerful thing you can do if this is holding you back is to learn to approve of yourself and let that be enough. Recognize when you have done something praiseworthy and make it a mission to treat yourself well when you do. Try to allow yourself to talk about your accomplishments even when you think they pale in comparison to your peers. Most importantly, learn to view other people's accomplishments with a positive attitude rather than allowing yourself to feel jealous, insecure, or judgmental. When it comes to conversation, being gracious toward others is an important skill, and one that will serve you well throughout life. Try to remember that other people's choices and accomplishments are not a comment on you and yours. Everyone has their own process in life and we all deserve respect in that regard. Don't allow yourself to be bitter or flippant. Recognize when you need approval and offer it to yourself. The more you do this, the more confident you will be around other people and the more others will approve of you.

Fear Of Embarrassment, Criticism, and Ridicule

There are very few people among us that aren't affected by negative or hurtful comments. Being criticized for your personal beliefs or having someone ridicule you for your shortcomings is rarely an easy thing to bear. Human beings are, in many ways, pack animals. We tend to do our best work when we are in groups. We all need the support and appreciation of others to some degree. Being ostracized from a group can be extremely painful and very difficult to overcome. This is particularly true for people with low self-esteem and/or an unrealized need for approval.

Unfortunately, adversity is a part of life and many conversations will lead to negative places, especially where work environments are concerned. If you offer an idea at a meeting or other gathering with your colleagues and they reject that idea, it can really hurt. And if you end up feeling embarrassed or regretful as a result, you're likely to shy away from offering ideas in the future. In the end, what could happen is that your fear of embarrassment might make it harder and harder to speak up. You could become so nervous about being criticized that you become withdrawn or unproductive at work. The same can be said for similar situations at home with your family or out with your friends.

It is important to remember that everyone experiences rejection and criticism in life. It is not an easy thing to endure but it shouldn't be allowed to conquer you. If your fear is making it hard for you to talk to people, it's time for a change. If you are afraid of being misunderstood, overlooked, judged, or saying something stupid, conversing with other people is bound to be difficult and anxiety provoking. Take some time to reflect on how these fears might be influencing your self-beliefs and causing you to avoid talking to people. It may be helpful to think about how others feel in the public situations. When you are in a group, remind yourself that everyone is vulnerable in exactly the same way you are. In fact, most other people are so focused on their own conversational mishaps to even notice yours. Reminding yourself of this regularly can be a powerful tool when it comes to living past your social fears. Everyone is more focused on themselves than they are on you or anyone else. It's only natural. Your embarrassment might not even feature on their radar!

Also remember that criticism can be helpful when it comes to refining your ideas and moving toward your goals. Knowing where you went wrong and how you could've done things better can be a great way to pave the way towards new skills, better knowledge, and all around self-growth.

If you find it difficult to cope with criticism ask yourself why.

Is it because of an ungratified need for approval?
Is it because receiving criticism makes you feel embarrassed, unworthy or incompetent?
Does criticism make you feel inferior to others?
How does it affect your self-esteem?

Seek to understand these things about yourself and try to keep perspective by imagining how other people feel in similar situations. If you know someone who copes with criticism very well, think about why this is or ask them if you can. In the future, resist the urge to put yourself down. Rather, try to get something positive out of your negative experiences. Try to learn something from them and move on. When it comes to ridicule or criticism that is designed to hurt you, tell yourself to let it go. That type of negativity will not serve you so it's best not to let it sink in too far.

Heightened Intelligence
It's hard to believe that intelligence can cause problems where communication is concerned. Surely the people who are the smartest should be the most socially savvy, right? Unfortunately not. The truth is, academic intelligence does most definitely *not* guarantee social intelligence. In fact, often the opposite is true.

Those who spend their lives working hard to achieve the highest grades in school and refining their chosen technical skills, often lack the social skills they need to actually benefit from these accomplishments in the real world. As an example, you may have seen someone at work advance to a high paid position quickly and effortlessly, regardless of the fact that they might have been less intelligent and less competent than you. You may have become angry or confused by a situation like this because your skills and knowledge far outranked that of the other person. It may have seemed extremely unfair. Yet this type of thing happens all the time and it's usually because the people who are claiming the career ladder are better at understanding the social side of things. They may have better people skills than you and it is these skills that ultimately lead to their success.

So what is it about being smart that could be holding you back from being a good conversationalist?

Firstly, *some* people who are highly intelligent fail to ask other people for their opinions, thus coming across as rude, arrogant, or self-obsessed. Secondly, some people with heightened intelligence lack a certain social sensitivity. They may be so sure of themselves on an academic level that they rarely give others a chance to speak, often ignoring, interrupting, or correcting them. A smart person may be highly critical of others or they may be emotionally insensitive. This can alienate them from others, making it hard to make or maintain friendships and causing them to be more of an outsider at work. I do not to mean to suggest that all intelligent people lack social skills! Such a statement would be wildly untrue and unfair.

However, there are some people with heightened intelligence who are completely socially inept. Often, the thing that increases this ineptness is a reluctance to recognize when they've said something wrong or to ask others for help where socializing is concerned. They might find it hard to admit that they need help with something other people find so easy. Smart people can be stubborn, so seeking guidance with something as basic as conversation can make them feel weak or inferior.

As I mentioned earlier, social skills take practice. If a person of high intelligence has not had the chance to learn and refine those skills, it's no great surprise when they fumble through conversations offending people and/or misreading social situations. Similarly, a person whose focus is placed entirely on logic may completely misunderstand other people's emotional experiences. It is immensely important to resist the urge to explain human feelings with logic. Humans are extremely complex beings, each of us carrying around years of personal experience, thoughts, and beliefs entirely our own. When we choose to reach out to another person to help us navigate an emotionally difficult situation, we rarely choose the person who's likely to reduce our problem into a logical equation. Rather, we choose those people who have a heightened *emotional intelligence* as they are likely to take our feelings into consideration rather than simply telling us to do this or do that. If you feel that your intelligence might be causing you problems socially, do not fear. Later in this book there will be plenty of helpful tips and practical skills that will help you overcome this struggle.

Limited Experience
Understanding why you are the way you are is an important part of self-growth and overcoming difficulties in life. If you are the type of person who has never really felt comfortable around other people, it is possible that your childhood may have lacked opportunities for you to practice your social skills. There are many possible reasons for this. You may have been brought up by a socially inept parent, for instance, or you may have grown up under the watchful eye of an overprotective parent who held you back from exploring the world around you. You may have been an only child or the type of child who indulged in more solitary activities rather than getting involved in team sports or group activities. If you were bullied or picked on in school you may have developed a certain wariness when it came to being around other people. Similarly, if you have been bullied or looked down on by friends, co-workers, lovers, or family in your adulthood, you're likely to experience a similar anxiety.

If your life has lacked social experience it's likely that talking to people will be daunting to some degree. It's important to think about your own individual goals and what you'd like to achieve as a conversationalist. Not everyone wants to be the life of the party; some of us simply want to be able to get through a meeting or a date without feeling panic stricken! For this reason, try not to put pressure on yourself to become something you don't actually want to be. Learning to talk to people is possible for anyone but sometimes it's best to think in baby steps. People are more likely to succeed and achieve their goals when their goals are realistic. If you set a number of small goals along the way to a larger goal, you're more likely to reach that larger goal than you would be if you'd tried to jump straight to it.

Try to set a few goals that you really want for yourself. If your goal is to gain conversational experience so that you can feel more comfortable when socializing, make sure your goals reflect that, rather than attempting to spontaneously become a great public speaker. Understanding who you are and what you want out of life is a vital part of self-growth. Often when we want more out of life, we can be a little too hard on ourselves and we might be unrealistic with goal setting; thus setting ourselves up for a fall.

Take some time to think about what it is that you really want to achieve and set your sights on those things. Resist the urge to try to become an entirely different person or to put yourself down when you're not like other people. Having limited social experience in your childhood does not have to affect you in your adulthood. Human beings have an incredible capacity for change and growth. It's never too late to gain that experience and become a more confident conversationalist.

Being An Introvert
There are certain personality traits that can leave us naturally predisposed to anxiety or difficulty socializing. Being an introvert is certainly one of them. This is not to suggest that people who are shy or naturally quieter than others always have trouble in this area. On the contrary, many introverts are entirely content with their lives and they have no problem maintaining strong healthy relationships with

others. However, there are people who find that their quiet nature can get in the way when it comes to conversation.

People with a naturally introverted personality often struggle with shyness and increased emotional sensitivity. They may be easily hurt by criticism as well as finding it hard to cope with failure and embarrassment. So too, they may find receiving praise and accepting positive attention in general, extremely difficult. Furthermore, introverts may find busy social situations like parties over stimulating or daunting, preferring smaller get togethers or one-on-one sessions with friends. People in this category may also find things like job interviews, dating and confrontation particularly difficult.

For introverts, feeling comfortable in conversations isn't always going to be easy. As a child, being introverted may have lead to being bullied or having a limited amount of friendships. A child like this may have been surpassed by their peers in areas such as team sports, extracurricular activities, and early experiences with sexual love. These people may shy away from risk taking and fail to grab opportunities throughout life. An interesting and common facet of being an introvert is having some level of contentment in being alone. There are very few other personality types that lead to such great comfort in one's own company. Although this contentment can be an exceedingly positive attribute, it could lead to avoidance and reluctance when social situations present themselves, thus giving the introvert little to no practice in the social arena.

If you are an introvert it's important to know that this personality trait is not a fault or flaw. In many ways, it can increase your ability to self-sooth and to find a sense of inner peace. However, if you have a hard time talking to people, it would be wise to get out and practice your social skills as often as possible, even if this means simply sitting across from a colleague at lunch or accepting more invitations to go out. It's important for all of us to break out of our comfort zones from time to time as doing so can really help to make us more rounded, accomplished individuals. As so much of life involves communication, having poor social skills can hold you back where you might otherwise have excelled. Try to start by making a conscious effort to socialize more often. If the ideas of parties or busy bars don't appeal to you, try something else like meeting a friend for coffee or going on a nice long walk with someone you trust.

Being Set In Your Ways
Often, the reason people have trouble socializing is that their beliefs are too rigid. If you are naturally outspoken and your mannerisms suggest that you are always right and/or that you have the answer to everyone else's problems, you are less likely to develop lasting relationships with other people. When it comes to conversation we all need the ability to be flexible. Relating to other people - and in turn, having people relate to you - requires empathy and respect. Healthy communication demands that we listen to one another, take each other seriously, and value everyone's opinions whether we agree with them or not. It is important to learn to *listen* to others and to be able to recognize the difference between healthy discussions and heated arguments. We must be aware of how our language, tone, and volume affect other people. In conversations, people feel at their most comfortable when they are being listened to and valued. Talking to someone who is bossy and loud is rarely enjoyable.

Similarly to people who are extremely intelligent, those who are too set in their ways may have problems getting people to like them. They may lack emotional intelligence, making people around them feel uncomfortable or upset when they talk about something they care about. Generally speaking, people don't like having discussions with people who don't listen to them or who are overly critical of them. Furthermore, if your friends, family, or co-workers know you to be inflexible, they are likely to feel like they have to tip toe around you, leaving you out of any conversations that may challenge your beliefs. For people in this category, learning how to listen, empathize, and respect the people you are talking to will dramatically improve your conversational success.

Try to remember that listening to other people's views does not mean that yours are any less important, nor does it mean that you agree with them. By keeping communication amicable, mutual, and respectful, people are more likely to value your ideas when you bring them to the table. When you're talking to people try to allow everyone to have a bit of conversational leg room. Otherwise they may feel attacked, unwelcome, and unsure about talking to you again in the future.

Difficulty Reading Social Cues
Understanding social cues doesn't come naturally to everyone. Though there are many people in the world that are naturally tuned in to social situations, others find it hard to read body language, facial expressions, and vocal tone. People who struggle in this way might say things that are inappropriate, failing to recognize the tone of a conversation or upsetting people because they have responded incorrectly to something they said. So too, a person who has trouble understanding social cues may not recognize when their conversational partner wants to stop talking about a particular topic. They might not recognize when someone is uncomfortable and they may be prone to saying things that are upsetting without knowing it. People like this might hang around when someone is trying to end a conversation, causing social awkwardness and discomfort. Conversely, they may think that people don't like them when in fact, they do.

Conversation can be extremely anxiety provoking for people in this category. They may find it hard to express themselves and therefore avoid social situations completely. Making and maintaining relationships may be hard for someone who is socially inept in this way, leaving them feeling isolated and ostracized. Furthermore, a person who can't read social cues is likely to have the same degree of difficulty when displaying social cues. Their body language might unknowingly contradict the message they are attempting to get across. They might avoid eye contact, making it seem like they aren't listening or as though they don't care what another person is saying. They may smile when talking about something sad. People like this are often misunderstood and this can be immensely frustrating for them and the people around them.

For these people, it may take a considerable amount of time and practice to learn how to read social cues. The practical skills I offer later in this book will be a great help, as they will guide you through issues such as body language, facial cues, and 'reading the room'. But you can learn these skills even more easily and productively by employing the help of a good support network. Having a close friend or relative "read" your body language when you are talking is a great way to learn what social cues you're putting out.

Similarly, having a friend attempt to communicate to you *without* words - i.e. just using their facial expressions and body language - can help you better understand these things as well. If you get a chance to do this type of role-play, try having a mirror close by too so that you can see what your conversational partner is seeing. As you embark on this journey of self-growth, remember to be kind to yourself. Try not to put yourself down or become frustrated if things take a little more time and effort than you anticipated.

Social Anxiety
It should come as no surprise that people who experience social anxiety are likely to find conversations daunting, intimidating, and emotionally activating. Social anxiety can affect so many aspects of life. From socializing to attending meetings at work to simply riding the bus. Furthermore, if you suffer from panic attacks due to social stimulation, going out can be petrifying. It's important to note that social anxiety is extremely common and as difficult as it may seem, it *is* something you can overcome. By learning how to slow your racing thoughts, gain and maintain perspective, and rationalize the situation at hand, you will be able to overcome this obstacle. Most importantly, although it may take time and perseverance, if you really want to overcome your fears, you will have to face them at some point.

If social anxiety and panic attacks are a major problem for you, try to give yourself plenty of time in order to recover from them and remember to be patient with yourself. Take one thing at a time. Facing your fears works best when it's done in baby steps. Throwing someone with extreme social anxiety into a busy party for instance, could be so overwhelming that it would likely increase their panic and discomfort. This is the type of thing that could be entirely counterproductive. A better way to approach this would be to start with something small like meeting a friend for coffee in a cafe where you feel at least reasonably comfortable. Make sure that this is a friend who is understanding of your fears and who would like to help you overcome them. When you feel your anxiety rising - when your heartbeat increases, you feel nauseous, shaky, or sweaty - tell your friend how you are feeling and rate that feeling with a number from 1-10; 10 being the worst anxiety you've ever felt, 1 being cool, calm and collected.

At that point, be sure to stay right where you are no matter how high the number is. You can continue talking to your friend or take some time to be quiet - whatever feels best to you - but make sure to resist the urge to get up and go to the bathroom or to leave the room entirely. Rather, stay where you are and a minute or so later, rate your feelings from 1-10 again. Usually at this point the number will have dropped or stayed the same. In some occasions it will have risen.

Regardless, stay where you are and do this a few more times, talking to your friend or simply being quiet. Gradually, you should see notice that your level of anxiety drops the longer you stay put. Try not to leave or get up from the table until the number has dropped below a 3 or 4. Doing this type of exercise regularly is a great way to start overcoming social anxiety and panic attacks. It's a method that will help you prove to yourself that even when you're panicking and your thoughts become catastrophic, you are actually fine, there is nothing to fear, and you will be okay.

Remind yourself whenever your anxiety begins to rise that you have felt anxiety before and you have survived it. The physical effects of panic attacks are merely a physical response to adrenaline. Remember too that anxiety is a natural and normal human process. It is an instinct linked to the survival of our species and in that way, you can think of it as a positive force! When anxiety is controlled it can actually be a very helpful part of life. Changing the way you think about anxiety can really help you get perspective and gain control over it.

For people who are crippled with panic attacks, it might be worth educating yourself about panic so that you can better understand the process at hand. Speaking to a professional about your panic attacks can also help dramatically. If you have friends or relatives who have suffered from panic, think about talking to them as well as this might help you gain some knowledge about it while making you feel less alone in your struggles.

Part Two: Learn How To Talk To Anyone!

Becoming a great conversationalist isn't just about being confident, speaking intelligently, and mastering the art of body language. Although these skills are an integral part of successful communication, if you really want to be able to talk to anyone, you'll have to truly understand what other people really want out of a conversation. Learning more about people and understanding what you can do to make them want to be around you will serve you much better than simply learning a bunch of generic tips and tricks.

It's important to note that it would be unrealistic for me to tell you that a small handful of knowledge could make you the most popular person in town, and the same can be said for overcoming social anxiety. These things take time, determination, and a lot of thoughtful reflection. The thing is, although learning basic social skills will be a big help, when it comes to matters involving other people, things tend to be a bit more complex than that. Every person you meet and every scenario you play out with them will be different to some extent. This is why it's wise to go a bit deeper when learning how to have successful conversations, rather than trying to fake your way through social situations and causing yourself added anxiety. Now, that being said, do not fear! Later in this book I will provide you with a plethora of skills that will come in handy in all sorts of conversations. But for now, I'm inviting you to think a little bit deeper.

Become The Conversationalist You Always Wanted To Be

Start by thinking about someone you know or have known in the past who always seems to have people around them. This does not necessarily have to be the most outgoing person on earth, the "life of the party", or the class clown. Rather, think more about the type of person who always has people sitting at their table at lunchtime or who seems to be out socializing all the time. Most of us know someone like this. In fact, most of us want to - and do - sit at that person's table at lunchtime!

But what is it about that person that makes us feel so comfortable, so *at ease* in their presence? What is it about the way they talk to people that makes us want to get closer to them?

Think about a person in your life who has qualities like this. If no one comes to mind, think about friends from your school days or reflect on character in a movie or a TV show that fits the bill. Try to think about why people want to be around this person. What is it about them that makes people want to confide in them?

Do they have any unique conversational skills?
Any special personality traits?

If you take just a moment or two to reflect on this, I'm sure you'll think of a few positive qualities they possess straight off the bat; things like openness, honesty, respect, and trustworthiness. You might think further about it and identify more qualities such as wit, a warm smile, a positive attitude, or a good shoulder to cry on.

As you can imagine, these are all great qualities when it comes to socializing. But more importantly, the one thing you can almost always say about a person like this is that they are *relatable*. They can empathize with just about anyone. They think fairly. They ask questions. They show a genuine interest in what people say.

When it comes to being a great conversationalist, it is qualities like these that far outweigh simply learning basic communication skills. For whatever reason, some people are more naturally able to tap into other people's needs than others. They are able to make people feel good about themselves, and they seem to know all the right things to say. The rest of us might need a little guidance where things like this are concerned. However, you can learn to harness some of these qualities by simply learning a few things about human psychology.

As you continue to read through this book, I want you to picture yourself the way you'd like to be around other people. Take a moment now to close your eyes and visualize yourself happily conversing with other people.

Imagine yourself feeling comfortable and confident. You may not want to be like the person I described above. Instead, you might imagine yourself with having a few new friends, talking comfortably to a lover or partner, or you may see yourself having the conversational savvy to confidently climb the career ladder; whatever it is that will make *you* happy.

Keep this image in your mind as you read on. Think about the people you want to talk to and how you can put the information in this book to good use. As I've said time and time again, as human beings, we are all different. Who you are, what your past was like, and what you want out of life, are all things that are unique to **you**. It's important to keep that in mind when reading a book like this. Remember that the aim is not to become someone new. The aim is to become the best version of yourself. This is your journey so be sure to periodically take time to think about yourself, your life, and your goals in order to get the most out of it!

The Secret Trick That Makes Conversation So Much Easier!

As complex as human beings are, there are certain things that all of us need. We all need food, water, and sleep. Beyond our physical needs, there lies a number of secondary needs that almost all of us have in common. These are often known as our *fundamental needs*.

As children, we get most of these things from our parents, guardians, and teachers, but as we grow up we usually acquire these things within ourselves and via the relationships we have with other people. For instance, we all need to feel safe and protected, we all need play and recreation, we need the opportunity for personal growth, we need a sense of control of our surroundings, and we need to feel that we are free (in many senses of the word). But in addition to these things, we also need to feel a sense of community and belonging. We need social stimulation, love, and affection. And most importantly, we need to feel a sense of importance. It is these last few things that I like to think of as our *conversational* or *social needs*.

In most circumstances, acquiring our social needs means talking to people in one way or another. We will feel a natural sense of importance when we are listened to and when people ask for our guidance or advice. We will feel that same sense of importance when people show a genuine interest in us, when they remember our names and ask specific questions about our lives. We get a sense of value within our community when we feel respected by other people. We feel a sense of belonging and increased self worth when we are asked for our opinions on important matters. And very often, we get a sense of love and affection through the conversations that take place when we're dating or in an intimate relationship. Through conversation we get to feel appreciated by our lovers. We get to feel understood and supported by our friends and family. We get to feel valued by our colleagues.

With all of those warm and fuzzy social needs still fresh in your mind, think of this as a golden rule, when it comes to conversation: do unto others as you would have them do unto you.

We have all heard this phrase at some point in our lives, though it is most commonly used in a cautionary sense; a thought meant to guide us away from mistreating others. In this context however, I want you to think of this rule in a positive sense. Think actively about what your conversational partner needs from you by thinking about your own social needs and what you want out of conversations. Think about how you'd like to be treated by other people. Then think about what you can offer someone else that will make them feel comfortable and happy in your presence. You now know that almost everyone on earth has the same social needs, so one of the best ways you can be a great conversationalist is by simply providing your conversational partner with some of theirs. Put simply, give the people what they want!

If our fundamental social needs are the thread that ties all together, then we already know at least a handful of things about every single person we will ever talk to. We know that they need to feel important. We know that they need to feel valued. We know that they need to feel a sense of belonging. All you need to do is figure out how to give them some of those things. Picture the person I described earlier at the start of this section, the one who people always want to be around, the person everyone wants to talk to. That person makes people feel important. They make people feel like they belong, like what they have to say is interesting and important. That is why their social calendar is always buzzing. That is why people feel so at ease around them.

Now, if all we had to do here was decode the mystery behind what people need from each other, I'd end the book now, but there's still plenty more to explore. What we've really just done here is stripped conversation and communication down to basics. We've exposed its bare necessities. It's important to think of conversation like this from time to time because often when we're talking to people things can seem a lot more complicated. Keeping these simple ideas in mind can make a mammoth difference for those of us who feel distracted, under-confident, and nervous in social situations. It can also help make your conversations more productive when there's a job to be done. It can help us understand and avoid conflict.

Consider this notion a reference point as you read on. Keep this knowledge at the front of your mind because knowing and understanding these few small truths about people will make learning how to talk to them a lot easier. Once you understand people, that is to say, once you've developed some extra *emotional intelligence*, you will be able to talk to absolutely anyone. You will be able to feel comfortable during a conversation and you'll be able to feel positive and confident afterwards.

Now that you've learned these fundamentals, let's take some time to focus on what *not* to do. Over the years, many of us develop bad habits and/or undesirable conversational qualities. These are things that have the power to repel people, annoy them, and make them uncomfortable. They are also habits that might be holding you back, things that are actually making you feel more nervous around people than you need to feel. Read the following list and try to identify any behavioral patterns that might be negatively affecting your conversations. Think of these things in light of everything you learned about providing others with their social needs so that you can find the connection between your bad habits and your difficulties with communication.

Breaking Bad Habits Forever

Get off your high horse
One of the most important things you can do to ensure successful and respectful communication is to be flexible and open to other people's ideas and opinions. Being bossy, loud, or forceful with your personal opinions can make people feel uncomfortable, annoyed, and angry. You might remember touching on this subject in part one when I highlighted the fact that being too set in your ways can be extremely damaging to a conversation. Being a know-it-all is a quality most of us can do without. And there is certainly something to be said about the importance of being humble. It is easier to relate to a person who shows some amount of weakness than someone who thinks or acts like they are perfect.

Think of conversation as a 50/50 experience. Everyone should get a chance to speak and everyone should take time to listen intently when others are speaking. When we talk to other people, we have to leave room for them to express their opinions and beliefs and we have to respect them regardless if we agree with them or not. Remember not to assume that everyone on the planet is going to agree with you 100% of the time!

You can recognize whether this is a problem for you by thinking about how people respond and react when you speak to them. If they spend long periods of not speaking, fidgeting, or looking around the room, something's probably wrong. If things get heated or aggressive, something is wrong. If your conversational partner isn't getting a chance to speak, something's wrong.

It can be difficult for people who are naturally ridged to learn how to be flexible. The problem is being inflexible isn't just going to upset the people you're speaking to; it is also likely to annoy and frustrate *you* as well. When it comes to matters of subjectivity, people will always have opinions that differ from yours. Berating them for these differences will not lead to any positive conclusions. Now, I am not suggesting that you simply sit and agree with everything everyone else says. That would be boring and could drive you crazy! Rather, I am encouraging you to value other people's opinions the way you would have them value yours.

Having a discussion about subjective ideas can be a very positive and intellectually stimulating experience when it is done on respectful terms. However, if there are subjects that are likely to make it hard for you to listen to other people's opinions, it's probably best to steer clear of them. If another person brings up a topic that you think could cause an argument, it is absolutely fine for you to politely suggest moving on to another subject.

Don't go on about yourself
Talking incessantly about yourself is the type of behavior that is bound to bore and annoy people. It's extremely important to be careful about this particularly bad habit. There is nothing wrong with talking about yourself and your accomplishments as long as it's done in a relevant, respectful, 50/50 manner. Similarly, if someone is asking you questions about yourself, it is absolutely fine to answer accordingly. The problem is not talking about yourself per say. Rather, the problem arises when you seem to talk about yourself more than anything else.

For instance, if you regularly change the subject in an attempt to get the spotlight back on yourself, people are likely to feel peeved about it after a while. Most people will enjoy the opportunity to talk about themselves and their accomplishments as well, so it's important to make sure you allow for a balanced exchange. Conversation should be a forum where everyone gets a chance to speak. Bragging or complaining too much will not make people want to talk to you.

Interrupting people and attempting to steer the conversation back to you is just rude.

Furthermore, do not simply sit and wait for your turn to talk. This will make it very apparent that you're only interested in what you have to say. People can tell when you're not listening to them and when you're disinterested. If you're constantly looking around the room yawning until the other person stops talking and then you jump straight in with an irrelevant story about yourself, it'll be pretty obvious that you don't care about what the other person was talking about. Cutting people off when they're talking just proves that you're not listening, thus making the other person feel completely insignificant. Don't be rude. As a general rule: *listen first, talk second.*

Choose your topic wisely
Talking about things that are upsetting, unnecessarily graphic, or generally thought of as inappropriate can make people feel very uncomfortable. Steer clear of subjects that might lead to distress or unease. Not only will inappropriate subject content be upsetting, it might put your conversational partner on the spot, forcing them to talk about things they might not want to talk about. This is something to keep in mind throughout the duration of your conversations but may be an especially helpful tip during awkward silences. If you tend to feel increased anxiety during silences, you might be prone to blurting out whatever comes into your mind next. This might lead you to say something you shouldn't. But if you find yourself panicking about what to talk about next, think before you speak!

Think about where you are and who you're talking to. For instance, if you're in a formal work meeting, don't try to break the ice by talking about sex or death. If you're on a dinner date, avoid talking about things that might gross your date out or make them feel insecure. Also, be careful not to put people on the spot by asking questions that are personal or private. As a general rule, don't ask people about their financial matters. If they want to tell you those things, that's up to them. Similarly, if you're not particularly close to someone, it's probably best not to ask them questions about their private medical issues or their love life.

Along a similar vein, be careful not to choose subjects that are completely irrelevant to the situation either. Let's say you're at that formal work meeting again and everyone is focused on work related issues. It's probably a bad idea to start talking about sports or your new car. As a general rule of thumb, keep conversations relevant and light unless you're absolutely sure that the topic you want to bring up will be received openly and easily.

Don't lie
When it comes to talking to people, honesty is the best policy. Always. This is especially true if you are embarking on a new relationship, friendship, or career path. Deception can create a seriously rocky foundation for new relationships at it's something that can (and usually will) backfire. There are many people in this world that lie when they're uncomfortable or when they're feeling inferior. Some people can't even seem to control it. They might exaggerate the truth a little bit here and there, pretend they know what someone else is talking about when they don't, or just come out with full-fledged lies. If this is a habit of yours, the quicker you stop it the better. If someone is talking about something that you don't have any experience with, rather than pretending to know what they're talking about, the best thing you can do is to ask them to tell you more about it.

This way you are being honest about yourself and your experience but more importantly, you're exhibiting two very important conversational qualities: **1)** that you aren't afraid of being vulnerable and **2)** that you're interested in what they're talking about.

By asking questions on the topic, you are making them feel important and useful, thus providing them with some of their fundamental social needs. In the end, both parties will benefit from a conversation like this because not only will that person feel better about themselves, but you will also have learned something new. You may find it hard to believe but most people prefer conversing with those of us who aren't afraid of admitting our shortcomings and limited experience rather than talking to someone who acts like they know everything. In addition, by being honest you will have likely succeeded in having a more balanced 50/50 conversation, one that is more likely to lead to continued positive communication in the future.

Don't worry about what to say next
When someone is anxious or nervous, it's usually written all over their face. They may fidget or avoid eye contact. They may look distant or uninterested. Often this is because the person is so uncomfortable in the situation that they can't focus on the conversation at all. Instead they are thinking about what they can say next or which direction they can take the conversation in. Getting into thought cycles like this can cause your nervousness and stress levels to rise.

You might end up in such a panic that you don't hear a word the other person is saying. If this is the case, you might miss something important and accidentally offend or confuse them when the conversation volleys back to you. Remember, it's okay to let the room breathe. You don't have to speak immediately when the other person finishes a sentence. Taking time to breathe and relax will make you look and feel more comfortable.

If you're regularly worried about what to say next, one of the best ways you can tackle this is by simply focusing on the other person and listening to them. If you are listening intently to what another person is saying, you will naturally know what to say when the ball is back in your court. And if for some reason you don't, it doesn't have to be a big deal. It is fine to say something like, *"wow, I'm not sure what to say about that!"* or to just jump in with a few questions. Ask the other person to elaborate on the subject or ask how they feel about it. If there was something specific about what they were saying that you found interesting, ask them to talk more about that.

Generally speaking, people like to talk about themselves and their interests, so as long as your questions are appropriate, relevant, and sincere, you really can't go wrong. If you did accidentally become distracted while the other person was speaking, it's okay to admit that and ask them to repeat themselves. Remember, being a good conversationalist does not mean being a robot, you're allowed to have flaws and vulnerabilities; it is actually these qualities that people find the easiest to relate to.

Don't over prepare for conversations
Over preparing is similar to not worrying about what to say next but it's a habit that comes with its own downsides. Spending a lot of time preparing for upcoming conversations can backfire in a number of ways. First of all, the more time you spend agonizing about what to say before a conversation takes place, the more nervous you're likely to be when it actually happens. It can put a lot of unnecessary pressure on you. Being prepared to some extent is absolutely fine and can be extremely helpful. For instance, if you have a job interview coming up, preparing some potential answers is usually a good idea.

Similarly, if you're meeting someone new and you only knew a few facts about them, you might prepare a few relevant questions to break the ice. However, there is a fine line between being prepared for a conversation and psyching yourself out! If you prepare too much, you might be completely thrown off track when the conversation heads in a different direction than you anticipated. It's sort of like studying for a test and then getting to school only to find out that nothing you studied is even on it.

Try to have confidence in yourself before going into a new or challenging experience. Rather than memorizing lines, remind yourself to *listen* and *engage* with the conversation. Remember to breathe. If you're in a friendly meeting, it's okay to admit that you're feeling nervous. If you start panicking during the conversation, rely on asking questions and listening to the answers so that you can calm down and regain focus. The thing to remember here is that spending too much time preparing for a conversation can be a quick way to make a mountain out of a molehill.

Remember that conversations are not like making public speeches, they're a two way street! You don't have to perform or feel like you're under pressure. Try to embrace the fact that a conversation might take you into new and interesting territory. Embrace the unpredictability of it. And always remember that everyone is in the same boat.

Don't be judgmental
Judging people is a negative and offensive habit. It is not something that will serve you well where conversations and relationships are concerned. In order for a conversation to flow easily, all parties need to feel safe and respected. Judging or criticizing people can make them feel uncomfortable, attacked, and defensive; three things that can take a conversation to an ugly place or grind it to a complete halt. Remember, there is a difference between having a respectful discussion and arguing. You must leave room for people to be themselves. Respecting people's views does not necessarily mean that you agree with them, it simply means that you are open to hearing about their experiences with a fair and empathetic ear.

Furthermore, there are times when it's just better to let things slide. If you don't like the outfit someone is wearing, is it really necessary to comment it? If someone tells you about how they handled a situation at work and you would've handled it differently, is telling that person going to help them at all or just make them doubt themself and feel embarrassed?

Think about how productive your thoughts about others are before sharing them, especially when it comes to things that are important, personal, or things that you have no experience with. It is entirely natural for human beings to feel differently about things. Judging someone or being nasty to them can make you seem closed minded, unreasonable, hateful, or bitter. It is a negative habit that could make people feel reluctant to be around you.

Everyone's life is different and the choices people make are not a reflection of the choices you make. Allow people their opinions and experiences, and they will allow you yours.

Leave something to the imagination
Sometimes when you're talking to a new person or when you're particularly nervous, you might find you lost control of the conversation. This could lead to you saying things that are inappropriate or simply talking too much on any given subject. You might find yourself spending twenty minutes talking about something that could've been summed up in two, or you might unnecessarily describe every little detail about something that's best discussed in a simpler way. It's normal to be nervous when talking to certain people and it can be hard to keep hold of a conversation; however, it's important to leave some things to the imagination.

If you have a tendency to babble out of nervousness, try to remind yourself to pause, breathe, and listen throughout your conversations. Try to recognize when you might be taking the conversation into negative or inappropriate territory. Notice when you've been talking about the same thing for a long time and either change the subject or allow the other person to talk.

Unless you are absolutely sure that you're in the right company to discuss heavier topics in detail such as sex, death, serious illness, financial matters, or criminal activity, try to keep it brief or steer clear of these topics completely. Similarly, be careful about talking passionately about politics as this may trigger negativity and arguments. Sometimes, less is more. Be careful not to rant about things or complain a lot. There will be times when you will be in the right company to discuss negative subjects so you don't necessarily have to avoid them entirely. As a general rule, if you feel 95-100% sure that broaching a heavier topic will be received well, go for it. If not, stick to lighter topics.

Remember as well that, sometimes it's best to get to the point rather than going on and on about something another person might find boring or unnecessarily time consuming. This is especially true in situations where you need to be productive and get things done. Whatever the situation, when you recognize yourself talking endlessly or just saying too much about one particular topic, try to tell yourself to conclude what you're talking about and ask the other person some questions so you that you'll have a chance to calm down while they're speaking.

Don't fidget
Whether you're in a one-on-one conversation, a meeting, or a social setting with a group, try to be mindful of what your hands are doing. Fidgeting not only makes you look nervous and under-confident, but it can also make the people around you soak up that nervous energy and become distracted. When you're speaking the focus should be on what you're saying, not what your hands are doing.

Furthermore, when someone else is speaking, they should feel that you are engaging with them and that you are listening with genuine interest. Fidgeting can make you look bored or disinterested. The same rule applies to any "props" you may have around you such as a pen, a coffee cup, the zipper on your jacket, virtually anything that your hands may reach out for when you're feeling a bit uncomfortable. Clutching onto props, lifting them up and down, spinning them round on the table, all of these things are distracting and could make you look as nervous as you feel.

The next time you are comfortable and relaxed at home, take a moment now and again to check in with your body. Notice your posture and take note of what your hands are doing. They might be lightly resting on your lap or a table, they might move slowly with the natural motions of your body. These are your body's natural positions, how your body looks and feels when you are at your most comfortable; a great resource when it comes to mastering your body language. When you are conversing or you're in a social situation, aim to use your hands more like you do when you're relaxed so as to look as calm, collected, and at ease as possible. Basically, using your hands to get a point across can make you look very natural and relaxed, picking or biting your nails and hanging on to props for dear life will not.

Know when NOT to talk

There are certain times when it's best to keep quiet. Recognizing these situations can be particularly difficult if you struggle to read social cues or if you tend to chatter when you're nervous. There are no set rules when it comes to things like this so it might be necessary for you to learn how to "read the room". On the most basic level, when you're involved in a conversation, don't interrupt the other person every time you have something to add. Being a good listener is equally important as being a good speaker. So too, try not to offer your opinion on things you have no experience with. It's okay to respond with questions and ideas. Your conversational partner will almost always prefer you having you say, *"that's interesting, tell me more about that"* than acting like you're an expert on something you're not.

Remember, people need to feel important and interesting. Asking questions not only provides them with that need but it also prevents you from saying something that might make you look desperate or poorly informed.

Also be careful about striking up conversations with strangers, especially in confined spaces. For instance, if you are in an elevator, on a bus, or waiting in line at the grocery store, you are likely to be physically close to people you don't know. Most people in these situations will be thinking about things that do not involve having random conversations and it's usually best to leave them alone!

They may be thinking about where they're going next or mentally ticking things off their to-do list. They may be getting some much-needed quiet time or they may be having a bad day. Although there is nothing wrong with a polite "excuse me" if you need to get past them or a simple smile and "hello", trying to initiate a full fledged conversation with strangers is usually a no go. If however, the other person starts talking to you first and you feel comfortable entering the conversation, it is fine to do so as long as your behavior matches theirs.

For instance, there are times when someone might say something to you first but they are not actually trying to initiate a full conversation. They might just want to tell you that they like your shoes or they might only be asking you for directions. These times usually call for brief responses. If the other person continues talking to you or they start the conversation with an open-ended question about you then that may be a sign that they will be happy to engage in a brief conversation.

One thing that is important to note is to be careful when conversing to people who are working in customer service; i.e. the waitress serving you lunch, the barista at a local cafe, or people working in stores. While these people may ask you questions and seem genuinely interested in talking to you, it's important to keep your responses brief and remember that this is part of their job. If you talk too much with these people you might be keeping them from their work and that can make them feel awkward and uncomfortable. In situations like this, keep your exchanges brief and polite.

Overcoming Difficult Thoughts and Feelings

If you've struggled to talk to people part of or all of your life, then you are bound to have developed some negative feelings and anxieties about social situations and communication in general. It is understandable. These might be things that are rooted in your self-esteem, feelings of self-worth, and your sense of self as a whole. However, there are many people who develop social / conversational anxiety later in life. You may have been very comfortable socially in your earlier days but feel the opposite way now. There are many reasons changes like this can occur such as going through a period of transition, having a traumatic experience, experiencing depression or anxiety, losing your job, going through a break up, losing a friend or family member, coping with financial struggles, and virtually any other difficult change in life.

Events like these can completely alter the way we feel about ourselves and the world around us. They can cause a dip in your self-esteem, a rise in anxiety, and feelings of reluctance or inadequacy where socializing is concerned. In this section, I will touch upon a few common underlying difficulties that can make talking to people especially difficult.

Whether you have struggled with communication your entire life or you have recently developed this type of anxiety, chances are there will be some underlying fears and negative thoughts that are making conversation particularly troublesome for you. Low self-esteem and negative self-beliefs are some of the most common underlying problems that can make it hard for people to converse with others. Unfortunately, they can also be some of the most difficult things to overcome. If this is something you struggle with, you might have developed an inner voice constantly telling you that you're not good enough. You might have a habit of judging yourself too harshly. You might become paranoid about how other people are perceiving you. If you're susceptible to harmful thoughts like these, you might find it especially hard to recover from mistakes, social faux pas, and embarrassing moments.

For instance, if you say something that came out the wrong way, you might be too hard on yourself about it. You might internalize it or exaggerate the severity of it in your mind. You might indulge in mental reruns of that moment, playing it over and over in your head rather than brushing it off and moving on. These kind of problems can lead you into patterns of avoidance, meaning that you're more likely to avoid potential pitfalls rather than facing them head on. You might choose to stay in rather than going out for the night. You might steer clear of dating altogether. You might decide not to apply for a job or promotion because your fear of talking has become bigger than you. The problem is that the more we avoid social situations and/or assertive communication, the harder these things will become. Each time you choose to cancel your plans and stay in for the night, you're reiterating your fear - *feeding* it - and ultimately making things harder on yourself.

No matter what type of life you've had, the experiences you have lived through will have played a big part in shaping who you are and how you view yourself among other people. Low self-esteem can force us into habits of thinking poorly about ourselves. If you feel inadequate or unworthy, it's no wonder you feel nervous when speaking to people. As I mentioned earlier, overcoming low self-esteem is possible but it does take practice and determination. Unfortunately there is no quick fix for things like this, but there are things you can do every day that will change your self-beliefs little by little.

Start by simply treating yourself kindly every day. Do something nice for yourself as often as possible - ideally once or more every day - and remind yourself each time that you're doing these things because you *deserve* them. Whether it means buying yourself something nice, taking a relaxing bath, or going out for a walk on a sunny day, as long as what you're doing is just for *you*, you're on the right track. Little things like this may seem insignificant and even a bit silly at times but the more you do them - the more you actively treat yourself with respect and love - the more your self-esteem will naturally begin to rise.

In addition to this, start making an effort to listen to your inner thoughts throughout the days and recognize when you're being unfair or unkind to yourself. Try to identify any thought patterns you have that might be holding you back in life. If you're avoiding social situations or other events that require you to talk to people, think about what underlying self beliefs are causing you do to so. Negative self-talk will not serve you in any way; it will only keep you feeling awkward and inadequate. It will make it very hard for you to live the life you want and to be the person you want to be. Low self-esteem can hold you back from taking risks and following your dreams. If you hear yourself thinking, *"I'm not good enough to apply for that job"*, *"No one will ever love me"*, *"I'll never be able to have what other people have",* or any other negative mantra, make a resolve to stamp it out! You have to practice stopping those thoughts in their tracks and turning them around if you ever want to overcome your negative feelings about yourself. These things will take time but it's important to keep chipping away at those unhelpful self-beliefs. Eventually you will start feeling better about yourself. Little by little you will start to see an improvement to your feelings of self-worth.

Another common underlying difficulty people experience when talking to others is panic and anxiety. If you experience panic attacks, social situations might fill you with dread but overcoming panic is actually easier than you think. There are many ways to rid yourself of panic attacks including taking a course in mindfulness and meditation or talking to a professional who focuses on cognitive behavioral therapy. But not everyone needs help from a professional to learn to beat panic. You can start by understanding what panic attacks really are. With knowledge comes power. When you are in a state of panic your body goes into "fight or flight" mode. This is a natural part of human life and it is one of the most *beneficial* physical responses we have. Fight or flight gives us the adrenaline rush we need to protect ourselves in dangerous situations. It causes our heart to race, we might sweat and tremble, we may feel too hot or become nauseous, lights may suddenly seem too bright, we might feel confused or over stimulated, and most often we feel an extreme desire to flee the scene. But all of these things are nothing more than a chemical response.

The problem arises when our bodies go into fight or flight mode unnecessarily. For whatever reason, we perceive danger in situations where they might not be any danger at all. For instance, you might experience panic attacks on the bus or in a busy shop. As your panic rises and your body begins to react to the adrenaline, it is hard not to notice subtle changes in how you feel physically. You may become a *super scanner*, mentally scanning your body for these physical changes, becoming focused on them and allowing yourself to be convinced of all sorts of catastrophic ideas such as "I'm having a heart attack", "I can't breathe", "I'm going to pass out or be sick". But the fact is that most of these catastrophic thoughts never even come close to fruition. Rather, these thoughts are likely to cause you to feel even more fear and panic.

Learning how to stop *super scanning* is a vital part of letting go of your panic attacks. When you feel those changes in your body, you must tell yourself that this is nothing more than a chemical response. These changes are really nothing more than a misunderstanding between your thoughts and your body. When you finally cease to be afraid of these physical changes, you're far more likely to decrease the duration and the severity of your attacks. Realize that you have control over your mind and your body.

Another great skill to have when it comes to gaining control over panic is to *look at the evidence*.

For example, if you are on the bus when your panic rises, ask yourself a few questions such as "Have I felt like this before? Did I die? Did I cause a scene? Did I survive?".

In most cases, you will be able to recognize that you *have* felt like this before and that you *did* survive. You might be able to note that you have felt this way many times before and although those times may have been exceedingly unpleasant, they were not symptoms of any major health issues and you did get through them. The more you think like this, the more you will begin to recognize that in most of these situations there is in fact, nothing to be scared of. You may also benefit from asking yourself "what's the worst thing that could happen?".

Let's say you're back on the bus. What is the worst thing that can happen? You might get off the bus a stop early or you might be uncomfortable for the entire journey. At the worst (though it is actually extremely rare) you might be sick. What will happen then? Will people judge you or laugh at you? Might they actually be concerned for you or offer you help? Asking yourself questions like this is a great way to battle your panic with calm logical thinking. This way of thinking can redirect your dizzying thoughts and remind your body that there is no danger, no necessity for all that extra adrenaline.

Finally, it's important to recognize if you have a habit of avoiding situations that might cause you to have a panic attack. In many circumstances, the thing that people are actually afraid of is panic itself; a fear of fear, if you will. Avoidance is rarely ever a good thing. The only purpose it serves is to reiterate your anxiety and make you more and more afraid of situations that are actually harmless. If it's social anxiety that causes your panic attacks, avoiding social situations will only make things worse. The fact is, you might feel a bit nervous and panicky when you first arrive somewhere but it's important to remember that A) your anxiety might be quite intense when you arrive but it will gradually decrease the longer you stay in the situation and B) many other people in the same room will be feeling the same anxiety. Tell yourself that you are stronger than panic attacks. You deserve to be free of them. Don't let anxiety rule your life.

Other obstacles you might face in social situations are shyness and fear of embarrassment. Remember that many people are simply shy by nature and there is nothing wrong with this. We can't all be extroverts. Where shyness becomes a problem is in situations where you might be holding back when you need to be pushing forward. For instance, if you really want a promotion, being too shy or soft spoken might mean losing out to another, more confident candidate. But there are plenty of introverts in the world who get just what they want out of life. Encouraging yourself to harness some bravery where these things are concerned is vital. You may not be the most wordy of your competitors and you may not wish to be the life of the party, but if you have the skills and knowledge it takes to get ahead, there is no reason why you shouldn't try. Certain things in life make everyone nervous.

Job interviews, public speaking, dating; these things can be daunting for **anyone**. Try not to let your shyness evolve into avoidance or deeper feelings of low self worth. Being shy does not make you less able or less deserving of the things you want in life. It does not make you inferior to anyone else. Shyness is nothing more than one little hurdle. And we **all** have hurdles to jump in life.

When it comes to coping with embarrassment and fear of embarrassment, it's important to note that everyone deals with these things at times. The fact is, when we do or say something that we feel embarrassed by, a lot of the time these things actually go unnoticed by the people around us. This is because in social situations, most people are far more focused on their own potential embarrassment to even notice your awkward moments. Embarrassment can be a toxic force in our lives. It can hold us back from risk taking and deplete our self-esteem. Almost all of us have a tendency to indulge in imaginary reruns of our embarrassing moments. They can be like ghosts from the past creeping up on us, reminding us of times we did or said something stupid, causing us added stress and anxiety when we need to feel our most confident. Other times we might be reminded of our past embarrassments in the wake of a new one. It's almost a way for us to kick ourselves when we're down and it's an extremely harmful and unproductive habit.

Embarrassing moments that occurred in the past are best left in the past. They will not serve you in the present or the future. Try to forgive yourself for your past faux pas and move on. When it comes to fear of embarrassment, do your best to let that go too. Try to live in the moment rather than reveling in the past or pushing yourself into an unpredictable future. Embarrassment and worry are a waste of your time and energy. Remember that embarrassment is just a part of human existence. It's not a nice feeling but it's also not the end of the world. Go easy on yourself in moments of embarrassment. Try to laugh at it and let it go.

When it comes to coping with difficult thoughts and feelings in general, it's important to be kind to yourself. Putting yourself down or using your personal obstacles as a way to beat yourself up is a very harmful habit. Everyone has weaknesses and insecurities. If you are susceptible to be being overly hard on yourself, you can start getting rid of that habit by treating yourself how you would treat a friend. If a friend came to you for advice or a shoulder to cry on, would you put them down for their shortcomings? Probably not. (Hopefully not!)

You're more likely to listen to them and offer them some words of encouragement. This is how you have to treat yourself.

Similarly, in order to avoid excess nervousness in social situations, try not to focus too much on yourself and the possibility of failure. If you struggle to engage in conversation because of negative thoughts and feelings, try focusing your attention on the people you're talking to rather than focusing on your nervousness. Allow yourself to be curious about how they might be feeling in the situation. Remember that even when people look confident, they might be riddled with anxiety. When you feel your thoughts racing into harmful territory, try asking questions and really listening when people are talking. This way your mind is more likely to be occupied with the conversation rather than focusing on your anxiety.

Through all of this, try to maintain perspective. At the end of the day, there's only so much harm that can be done by an awkward conversation. Try to let yourself be light and actually enjoy social situations rather than thinking of them in a purely negative light.

Remember to forgive yourself if you say something embarrassing or if you succumb to a panic attack. Things like this are difficult to overcome so try to be a good friend to yourself rather than being your own worst enemy.

Striking A Balance
As I mentioned earlier, people are much more likely to enjoy talking to you if they are given the opportunity to acquire some of their

basic social needs during the conversation. This is not to say that you have to spend the duration of every conversation trying to make another person feel important and approved of. If you did that, it's unlikely that you'd enjoy conversations at all! But evidence suggests that you will be a much more successful conversationalist if you keep those fundamental social needs at the forefront of your mind.

Doing so could mean the difference between having a decent conversation and having a highly enjoyable and productive conversation. Thinking of those basic psychological needs can also help you keep your cool if you're conversing with someone you find to be intimidating difficult.

Conversations, and relationships in general, work best when they are balanced and when each party gives and takes in equal amounts. Remember that conversations can and should be enjoyable. They needn't be stressful or exhausting. But it is worth noting that you could be more likely to receive some of your own fundamental social needs if you're willing to supply others with theirs. Most things in life involve some give and take, especially where other people are concerned. You do not have to bend over backwards to make sure that the people you talk to are having the time of their life; especially if you're having a miserable time! In many social situations, you will have no obligation to please people who make you feel bad about yourself.

But at the same time, understanding these basic parts of human psychology is a great way to get people on your side. People will want to spend more time with you if they feel good after being around you. They will think more highly of you if they are given the opportunity to feel more highly of themselves when in your presence. Focusing on making people feel important and approved of is also a great way to 'reset' a conversation that's not going very well. By simply asking someone to elaborate on a topic, you are showing a genuine interest in what they're saying, thus giving them a chance to feel better about themself.

I have talked about having 50/50 conversations a few times in this book so far. What I mean when I refer this is not just that each party gets to speak an equal amount. It also means that each person gets a chance to be listened to and to feel like what they have to say is valid and valued. But 50/50 conversations don't stop there. I also like to think of this on an emotional level. There are people in this world that can be difficult to talk to and emotionally draining. Conversations with people like this can leave you feeling emotionally depleted and exhausted. A healthy conversation is one wherein each party leaves feeling as though they have maintained or increased the energy levels they had going into the conversation.

Now, in this particular aspect of conversation you will have little, if any, control over what the other person is saying. If you talk to someone who leaves you feeling drained, you might want to consider having fewer or shorter conversations with them in the future. However, you can change your own behavior to prevent leaving other people feeling drained by you. Be aware of how you are affecting people when you talk. If it seems like someone is starting to feel weary or bored by your subject content or if they seem like they're being affected by your negative energy, try to turn it around.

Take note of subtle changes to their face and body language. If the person you're talking to is silent for long periods of time this might be an indicator that they're not really into what you're talking about. If they are looking away a lot, fidgeting, or touching their face, hair or neck, this is usually a sign that they're uncomfortable. If you see their body leaning or turning away from you, this could mean that they're not enjoying the conversation. These are important things to keep in mind if you want to ensure that your experiences with others are more emotionally balanced.

When someone leaves a conversation feeling good, they will remember you in a positive light. This could lead to further positive experiences with them in the future. So too, it can help you feel more confident in all your passings with others. After you've had a conversation, take some time to reflect on it. Think about what went well and what didn't.

Did you have a good time?

Do you think the other person had a good time?
Were there certain topics that made your conversational partner seem enthusiastic?
Were there topics that seemed to make them uncomfortable?
Do you think this person would want to converse with you again?
Would you want to talk to them again?
 Why or why not?

Taking time to reflect like this is an active way to learn from your own experiences. By doing this you will be able to better recognize how you are being received. You'll know more about people and more about yourself. Most importantly, you will be able to perfect your conversational skills in order to have more successful conversations in the future.

Before moving on to part three where you will learn a host of conversational skills, I'd like to close this section by focusing your attention on a very short recap of what people want from conversations.

These things are worth keeping in mind as they will not only make people want to be around you more, but they can also act as a 'reset' button when your conversations take a turn for the worse. They are things that are especially helpful when talking to people who you may find intimidating or difficult to talk to as well as those whom you wish to think highly of you.

Below is a short list of key points for you to refer back to anytime you need a quick reminder.

10 Things People Want From A Conversation

1.) To feel important.
2.) To be approved of.
3.) To be affected positively.
4.) To feel valued and appreciated.
5.) To be remembered.

6.) To be listened to and understood.
7.) To be respected.
8.) To be empathized with.
9.) To be intrigued and delighted.
10.) To talk about things they care about.

Part Three: Simple Techniques To Improve Your Conversational Prowess

Now that we've covered all the reasons you might find conversation difficult as well as touching upon some important facets of the human psyche, this section is going to focus entirely on vital conversational skills. You have already read about a number of bad habits that might be causing your conversations to be stressful and unsuccessful. You have been encouraged to think about your past experiences and how they function in your present day life. And now that you are tuned in to your own obstacles and anxieties, you should be feeling ready to tackle some social situations.

In this section you will learn about mastering the art of body language and facial cues in addition to learning the top fifteen skills you need in order to become the conversationalist you would like to be. At the end of this section I will touch upon how to tackle some specific circumstances that you might find particularly stressful. Here you will learn about things like keeping your cool in job interviews, talking to people who intimidate you, making speeches and presentations, dating and making new friends, and how to deal with conflict and confrontation. By the end of this final section, you should feel confident about conversing with just about anyone.

Body Language
Body language is often thought of as the natural, unconscious movements we make to show what we're saying or feeling. However, this movement isn't just happening in our subconscious, it is something we can control and alter as we need to. As we encounter different social situations, our bodies have the power to enforce or negate any points we are trying to get across. They can help to reiterate our views, make people feel comfortable in our presence, and allow other people to accurately judge our reactions. For many people, these movements are so natural that they usually involve little to no thought at all. In fact, very few people in the world are actively thinking about what their body is saying while they're speaking or listening to someone else speak. But

understanding how body language works can be extremely valuable knowledge when it comes to being a good conversationalist.

Being able to use your body to effectively set and maintain the tone of your conversations can be a massive benefit and a great tool to have on your side. So too, being able to read other people's tone and mood by simply watching the way their body moves will help you "read the room" more effectively and prevent you from saying or doing anything embarrassing or inappropriate.

Rather than simply supplying you with a bunch of generic dos and don'ts, I think the best way to begin learning about body language is to do some experimenting with it. Don't worry, I'll give you plenty of tips and tricks as this section progresses but for now, as these things can be quite personal, you're likely to make far more significant progress by focusing on yourself and getting to know your own strengths and weaknesses.

To get a really good handle on body language, start by actively observing people who are engaged in conversation. Take note of any subtle movements they make as they converse. Note the tone of the conversation and see how their bodies react to different topics and phrases.

Are they having an enjoyable conversation?
Is the subject content happy and light?
If so, how is their body language conveying positive feelings?
Do they look calm and comfortable?
Are their shoulders relaxed or tense?
Are their shoulders slumped or chins dropped?
Are they facing each other or are either of them facing away from the other?
Is the tone of the conversation serious or sad?
How would you know this based on their body language alone?
Is one party tilting their head as they listen to the other?
Can you detect any movements that might suggest that one or both parties are uncomfortable?

This is a great and very valuable exercise to practice with close friends and family, as afterwards you will have a chance to talk about what you observed. Plus, it might be a bit inappropriate to stare at strangers while they talk!

Another great way to learn about body language is to watch people on TV or movies. Put a movie on and think hard about what the characters' bodies are portraying. Try to tune in to even the subtlest movements. Quiz yourself by putting the TV on mute and trying to figure out what the characters might be talking about by watching their body language alone. Try to notice any subtle shifts they make toward or away from each other. See if you can spot a moment when someone is listening intently, then try to recognize when someone looks like they'd rather be somewhere else. Ask yourself why you came to those conclusions. Think of any specific movements that might have led you to those beliefs.

When you feel like you're getting more confident *reading* body language, start trying to *speak* with it. Start by standing in front of a mirror and experiment with any positions or gestures you've learned from watching other people.

Think about something that is calming or relaxing and see how you hold your body as a result of those feelings.
Think about something that makes you angry, then something that makes you happy.
What changes in your body might someone pick up on if you were conversing with them?

Imagine the person in the mirror is someone you're uncomfortable around.
How might your body language reflect that?
Now imagine that person is someone you feel safe with.
What subtle changes do you notice about your body's positioning?

Getting to know your own body in this way is very important. Knowing that your body is conveying the message you want it to can take a lot of pressure and anxiety out of your conversations. Similarly, the better you become at reading and speaking with body language, the more likely you'll be to hide any nervousness you may be feeling when you're in high anxiety situations.

If you have a few close friends or family members that are willing to help, ask them if they might do a little role play with you. This doesn't have to be the most formal exercise on earth. It can actually be something very simple and subtle such as asking your friends if they think your body language can be a little confusing or if it conflicts with the tone of your conversations. After you have a conversation with them, ask them if they felt comfortable talking to you.

Ask if they thought anything your body was doing made them unsure of the tone you were trying to set. Ask them if there was anything specific that you did or didn't do that might've hindered or helped you make your point.

Remember that if you struggle with body language, these things will take some time and practice. There are plenty of people in the world who struggle with things like this. Unfortunately, difficulties like these might mean that you have to actively think about your body language rather than being able to trust your body's natural movements. However, the more practice you get, the easier and more natural body language will become.

During your practice sessions and/or any conversations you have with people that you're close to, practice *mirroring* your conversational partner. When they are speaking, look at their body and try to match the way they're sitting. For instance, if they lean in close to you, their body is telling you that they are actively engaged and interested in what you're saying. Reciprocating that by leaning in toward them will let them know that you are also interested and engaged in the conversation. If their legs cross toward you, this is usually a positive indication that they are comfortable with you and that they are happy in the conversation. You can express similar feelings by mirroring them and angling your body toward them in a similar fashion.

Mirroring is a very important part of body language. It is a simple and direct way of showing empathy and can therefore be a powerful skill to have under your belt. When your body moves in a similar way to your conversational partner's, they will feel like you are engaging with them and that you can empathize with how they feel. Mirroring is mostly beneficial for movements that you would class as positive and comfortable. They are usually easy to recognize and reciprocate.

However, *negative* mirroring is slightly more complicated. For instance, if someone is being confrontational or you are involved in a serious conflict with them, mirroring could exacerbate the situation rather than make anyone feel comfortable or calm. Imagine how someone who is becoming angry or irate might use their body. They might clench their jaw, raise their shoulders, point at you, shake their head, or rub their neck and shoulders. In a situation like this, if you mirror them, you could be perceived as being threatening.

As most people would rather avoid major conflicts, a good way to think of negative mirroring is this: if someone's negativity is directed *towards* you, it's probably not wise to mirror them. This could make you look as though you are inviting further conflict or a fight.

However, if someones negativity is directed *away* from you such as having a friend tell you about something frustrating that happened at work, mirroring them will not come across as aggressive or challenging but rather, it can be a nice way to show them that you're on their side and that they are justified in feeling the way they do.

To simplify: negative mirroring can be a positive action when it's communicating support and agreement. Mirroring someone who wants to fight you is just plain negative.

Now, it's important to note that you don't have to be an exact replica when mirroring someone! The aim is to simply try to move in a similar way while paying attention to the conversation and maintaining some degree of subtlety. Try not to concentrate so much on body language that you become distracted or lose track of the conversation. It's more important to listen than to mirror but mirroring can make people feel like they are in a safe situation where they can openly express themselves. After some practice all of this will feel much more natural. Remember how important it is for people to feel like they are being listened to and valued? Mirroring them is a quick and easy way to achieve this.

Mirroring can be especially beneficial in times of trouble. If someone is talking about something that is upsetting to them, mirroring them could make them feel understood, and respected, whereas moving your body in opposite ways might make them feel undervalued or rejected. Expressing empathy, via words and movement, helps make people feel like they are not alone. It's nice for people to feel like someone is on their side. As I mentioned just moments ago, mirroring can be a positive force during times when someone you know is experiencing a conflict that does not involve you. For instance, if your friend is going through a break up and they begin telling you about it, you can instantly express your empathy for them by simply mirroring their stance. Just be careful not to make it too obvious! You don't want to look like you're making fun of them or like you're lost in your own thoughts.

Mirroring is something that usually happens in a very natural, seamless way. You might notice that when you're really connecting with someone, your body might do this naturally without you even realizing it. Remember to listen to what your friend is saying and really engage with the story while you mirror them. This way you're less likely to think too hard about your body language and risk coming off as fake. Another thing worth mentioning when it comes to mirroring - and in fact, all methods of body language - is to keep your movements smooth and slow. If your body is jerky or you're rushing from position to position, you're likely to come across as nervous, disengaged, distracted, or uncomfortable.

When learning to master body language, there are a few basics you will want to keep in mind as much as possible. As I mentioned briefly before, leaning towards someone is generally thought of as a positive move while turning away from them is often perceived as negative. This means that generally speaking, turning to face your partner whenever possible will make them feel that you are engaging with them. You can take this even further by turning your chair to face them or repositioning yourself in a way that will make them feel like you really care about what they are saying. You might also achieve this by turning your feet in toward the person you're talking to as pointing your feet away from someone is a sign of discomfort.

Similarly, it's wise to avoid "closed off" positions such as sitting with your arms crossed or closing your eyes as these actions can make you look like you've disengaged, shut down, and wish you were somewhere else. Be aware of any objects that might be acting as a physical barrier between you. If you're sitting at a table make sure no books, centerpieces, laptops, etc. are blocking you. Shift these objects to the side if possible. If you're standing, try not to allow any furniture or other obstacles to get between you. And remember to always be careful about clutching onto objects like coffee cups and mobile phones.

When approaching any conversation - especially those involving work or other serious and/or difficult topics - try to adopt a confident posture. Be careful not to slump forward or focus your eyes on the ground or to the sides. Stand or sit with your back straight and your chin lifted. Relax your shoulders so that you look comfortable. A good way to practice doing this is by raising your shoulders as high as you can and then letting them drop down heavily. Imagine your shoulder blades being drawn down your back. This will not only make you look more relaxed but it will also cause your chest to push slightly forward, making you look confident and unafraid. You can also make yourself look more confident by taking up slightly more space than you usually would. You can achieve this by standing with your legs slightly parted or allowing your arms to be in a variety of open positions.

Leaning back in your seat can also make you look relaxed and confident however, leaning too far back may make you come across as bored or arrogant. Doing so may also make people think that you are a little too intense or even needy, so it's important to be mindful of this when attempting to adopt a confident position. Remember, all things are best in moderation!

Leaning slightly forward and slightly back in subtle ways can make you seem interested and interesting. Try not to stare at the ground or fidget, as these are motions that can make you look insecure or even frightened. The same goes for leg shaking, finger tapping, nail biting, and other unconscious distracting motions you might be making. Also, try not to let your arms flail about too much. It is okay to emphasize a point with hand gestures but try not to go overboard!

Be careful about touching your face, neck, or hair too much and resist fidgeting with your shirt collar or necktie. It's quite fascinating how motions like these can indicate that you are actually intimidated by a person or topic. Your neck is home to quite a lot of nerve endings. This is why having a sore neck or upper backache can cause you to have tension headaches as well as pain in your jaw and even your gums. This is also why having your neck and shoulders rubbed feels so good and relaxing. When human beings are anxious they will often unconsciously touch their neck in an attempt to physically soothe themselves.

Similarly, playing with your hair, rubbing your face, forehead, temples, eyes, and mouth also calm us down when we find ourselves in anxious states. Remember also to be careful with your props. I have already mentioned how fidgeting and creating barriers with them can send the wrong signals, but it is also important not to hold things in front of your chest or heart. Holding drinks, keys, books, etc. in front of your chest could indicate that you are on guard and that you're feeling threatened or scared. Remind yourself to lower objects or move them to the side so as to appear more confident.

Something you can do to appear more interested in what your conversational partner is saying is to nod along with them when they are speaking. This will act as a cue to let them know that you want to hear more. You can also show interest by tilting your head slightly or even resting your tilted head on your hand. This position is one of active engagement. It can be a simple way to make someone feel valued and important, thus providing them with some of their fundamental social needs and making them happy to be in your company.

For women, sitting with one leg tucked under your body while you face your conversational partner is actually a position your body might naturally adopt when you are feeling at ease in someone's presence. This is a position to be aware of whether you're the one sitting this way or the person you're talking to is. Keeping your eyes peeled for indicators of comfort and discomfort like this will help you navigate conversations and better understand the way your conversational partner is feeling.

One of the biggest issues when it comes to body language is eye contact. Avoiding eye contact and/or glancing back and forth is a sign that someone is distracted or uncomfortable. This is important to remember when it comes to your own actions but it is also a great thing to know when it comes to understanding other people's feelings. Glancing away a lot might mean that someone would like to change the subject or that they might like to go talk to someone else. Remember that, especially when you are out with multiple people, a conversation shouldn't make someone feel trapped. If you're in a group, it's okay to wrap up what you're talking about and allow the person to strike up a conversation with someone else.

When people are comfortably engaged in a conversation, they will naturally make eye contact with the person they are speaking to. But understanding how and when to make eye contact can be hard to figure out if you're not used to doing it. The first thing you want to be careful of is not to stare or glare at the person you're talking to.

Staring - that is, locking eyes with someone for and extended period of time - can make you look awkward or false. It might make someone wary of your intentions and could cause them to become confused and uncomfortable.

Glaring - that is, staring with a hardened facial expression - can make you look angry, disproving, or critical.

Remember, all things in moderation. When it comes to eye contact, more is better than less, but staring is a "no no". The aim is to appear interested and engaged, not threatening, condescending, or judgmental!

Finally, make sure that you respect other people's personal space. Standing too close to someone can make them feel anxious, threatened, and uncomfortable. It may also send the wrong signals such as implying romantic intentions. Be careful when touching other people as well. Many people are uncomfortable with physical contact so unless you know that someone wants to be touched, keep your hands to yourself. A light touch on an arm or shoulder can send a message of friendly reassurance but touching someone's legs, face, hair, neck, or intimate areas should be reserved for actual romantic encounters where these actions are desired and enthusiastically reciprocated.

Generally speaking, try to maintain a one to two foot radius of personal space and avoid being closer than that unless you are in particularly close quarters or you are certain that this will not make someone feel uncomfortable.

The Successful Conversationalist

Take a moment to think back on that idea of the type of conversationalist you'd like to be. Remember the person who other people want to be around. We know so far that one of the reasons people attract others is because they make them feel important and good about themselves. With the basic knowledge you now have about fundamental social needs, you are already well equipped to have more successful, enjoyable conversations. Your confidence may now be on the rise and you might be feeling a bit less intimidated than you were. But now it's time to go a step further. The following list will expand on some of the knowledge you've already learned in this book while providing you with fifteen advanced skills that will help get you ready to talk to anyone!

Top 15 Skills For The Great Conversationalist

1. Beware the Conversational Vampire

As you know, keeping a conversation equal and even is extremely important. No one likes to hang out with people who only talk about themselves. Nor do we tend to flock to people who are self-obsessed or emotionally draining. But in addition to that, it's important to keep your conversations light and lively. This means steering clear of serious and/or disturbing topics where possible but it also means keeping complaining to a minimum. Try to be as positive and upbeat as possible. Affecting people positively is a wonderful way to make new relationships, keep old relationships strong, and make conversions enjoyable.

Inevitably, there will be times when the tone of your conversations will be more serious such as in times of illness and death, political change, financial matters, and other major life changes. There will be times when you need to lean on your friends and times they will need to lean on you. But outside of these circumstances, it's important to let things be light. People will want to talk to you a lot more if you do.

2. Remember peoples names

I cannot stress this enough: Remembering people's names is extremely important! When you've only met someone a handful of times, addressing them by their name will instantly make them feel good about talking to you again. It will make them feel as though they had a positive and meaningful impact on you the last time you met. This in turn will give them the sense of importance and approval that we all crave. Knowing that you've remembered someone will make your conversation with them run a lot more smoothly rather than feeling like you're starting at square one again.

Furthermore, if you need to get a job done, calling someone by their name can make for a much more productive talk. People are more likely to want to help out knowing that you value them for who they are.

Forgetting someone's name can make things awkward and uncomfortable for both of you. If you are notoriously bad with names (as many people are), try making some notes about people when you meet them. You can do this on your mobile phone so that you can refer to it whenever you need to without looking suspicious.

Just make a note of the person's name, how you know them, and any other distinguishable qualities or interests they have. If you do run into someone and you're unsure of their name, you can either discreetly ask someone nearby if they know it or simply ask the person and apologize for forgetting. Then make a note about it so you don't forget next time!

3. Offer your full attention

I've said this time and time again but for good reason. Giving someone your full attention and listening intently when someone is speaking is an instant way to make someone feel interesting and important. Think of listening to someone as being a way of complimenting them. It's a way of telling them that what they are saying is fascinating and intriguing. Do your best to resist yawning, looking around the room, or repeatedly looking at the clock as these things can make you look impatient and disinterested. Reflect periodically on your body language to make sure that you look actively engaged.

Note that your arms are not crossed, that you're facing the person who's speaking and that you are leaning slightly toward to them. If you feel like your mind is drifting onto other things, try to refocus your mind and body back to the conversation. The aim is to make the person you're speaking to feel valued. You want them to know that you care about what they're saying. Often the best thing you can do is to put their needs at the top of your list of priorities and set any unrelated thoughts and feelings aside for the time being.

Before the arrival mobile phones, it was much more easy and more common to give people our full attention, but in todays world, our attention is almost always divided. In the wake of these societal changes, it's necessary for us to make a point of learning how to communicate with one person at a time. If your phone is likely to ring, ping, and ding with calendars, to-do lists, updates, emails, and shopping reminders the whole way through a conversation, something must be done.

Firstly, put the phone on silent, it's just common courtesy. Secondly, put it in your pocket or your bag. Having the phone on the table or in your hand while you're talking to someone is rude and distracting. It will make the person you're talking to feel like they're placing second in a race against your mobile device. If you are involved in a particularly serious or important discussion, put your phone on "do not disturb" mode so that it won't make any noise or vibrations. If there is some reason why you cannot do this - i.e. you're waiting for a *very* important call - inform the person you're speaking to at the start of the conversation. Express your apologies for keeping your phone on the table so the other person knows you do not mean to be rude. Then make sure that you don't pick it up again until absolutely necessary.

4. Be empathetic

Empathy is possibly the strongest and most important force in human interaction. Because the nature of human life is equally collective and individual - that is to say, we experience life as individuals as well as in groups - empathy acts like a bridge between the two. It has the power to validate our individual experiences and tie us to other people. Being able and willing to empathize with other people makes working and living with others easier and far more enjoyable. Most people would say that empathy is not something you can teach; it is something we are all born with to some degree. For people who feel an abundance of empathy, getting close to people can be emotionally painful and even disturbing at times. For those who feel a lack of empathy, people may think of you as rude or socially inept. As you can imagine, striking a balance where empathy is concerned isn't always easy.

If you naturally experience an abundance of empathy, your conversations are likely to be healthier than those who do not; however, for people in this category, it's important to recognize where other people end and you begin. It's natural to care for others but caring too much can cause you to put yourself on the bottom of your priority list. Taking on other people's troubles too much can cause you to become run down or overcome by compassion fatigue. You may have noticed at one point or another that empathizing too much can be exhausting and lead you to feelings of resentment. It can be hard to take care of yourself if you're constantly thinking about someone else and this type of relationship rarely ends well.

For this reason, make sure that you spend plenty of time thinking about yourself and recognizing the difference between caring for people and letting other people's problems take over your mind. Remember that 50/50 conversations are as much about you as they are about others.

If you have trouble feeling and expressing empathy, getting close to people might be especially difficult for you. You may remember me classing good conversationalists as being "relatable" and empathy plays a big part in that. If it's hard for you to feel empathy, the best way to summon it up is by imagining yourself in someone else's shoes. When someone is telling you about their day, imagine the events had happened to you and think about how you would feel in that situation. In addition to that, try to look and listen for any cues about how they might be feeling.

Are they smiling or frowning?
Is their voice light and playful or deep and grumbly?

Try to figure out what they're feeling and do your best to match it by telling them that you understand or offering them a simple nod of agreement. If you're still struggling to understand their feelings, it's entirely okay to ask them how they feel about the topic at hand. Sometimes all someone needs from you is validation. So by simply saying something like, "I understand. It sounds like that really upset you", you may be saying enough to feign empathy.

5. Be confident but cooperative

In order for a conversation to be enjoyable and successful, people should feel like they *want* to talk to you. That means being confident but not being cocky. Firstly, allow yourself to have a voice. Even if you're shy, try to express your opinions and say what you're thinking. Remember that it's okay to have opinions that differ from others and it's okay to talk about your own personal experiences. Often by just pretending to be confident, you will start to feel confident.

For those who are already confident but may be a bit pushy, remember that no matter how self-assured you are, people will still want you to ask them questions and listen to their opinions. They will want you to be interested in how they think and how they feel, not just hear your answers to every problem in the world. You can achieve a good balance by recognizing when another person wants to put in their two cents. If someone quickly raises their hand and then puts it down again, that's usually an indication that they have something to contribute. If someone keeps opening their mouth and getting cut off half way through a sentence, you should probably be quiet for a bit and let them speak. When someone else is talking, be sure to listen and wait for your turn to talk again. Don't talk over someone; conversation is not war, it's a way of bringing people together.

Knowing how to embrace differences is a powerful skill. People that seek to understand the views and experiences of others are almost always thought of has being understanding, empathetic, worldly, and easy to talk to. This does not mean you have to agree with everyone about everything. It means that you have to listen and value other people's ideas. If there are certain subjects that are too difficult to find common ground on, it might be best to agree to disagree and suggest changing the subject to something you can both agree on.

6. Allow yourself to be flawed
There's a lot to be said for being human. And by that I mean being a well-rounded individual with both strengths and weaknesses. Being a great conversationalist is not about knowing everything or being perfect. Pretending to be an expert on things you're not, can be cringe worthy and embarrassing. Going on and on about all the things you know and all the things you've done can be tiring for people to listen to. And, acting like you're the best at everything and like you have all the answers can get really annoying. It is much easier for people to respect someone who is honest, and that includes being realistic about your faults and flaws. All human beings go through ups and downs.

We all make mistakes; we all learn some things the hard way. All of us have to learn and grow throughout our lives and that might mean being seen in our less-than-graceful moments from time to time. Being able to admit your mistakes takes strength, but people will respect you for it. It is easier to impress someone by admitting you've done something wrong than pretending you did something right.

Most people know that no one is perfect and the sooner you know that about yourself, the better. You can learn something new and give someone else the feeling of importance they desire by asking them to tell you about the things you don't know a lot about. Asking for help with a certain skill can make you look humble while making someone else feel good about themselves. It's a win win. It doesn't matter if you're asking someone how to cook a certain dish or how they manage running a large business. The objective is to provide someone else with their fundamental social needs while making yourself look like an open, honest, appreciative person.

7. Ask the right type of questions

You know how important it is to ask questions by now, but what sort of questions are best? To start, unless you're in a close relationship or friendship with someone, don't ask questions that are overly personal or socially inappropriate. Those questions could easily cause more harm than good. First of all, you want to ask questions that are relevant to the conversation unless it's a good time to change the subject.

Second of all, you want to ask about things that won't make anyone feel uncomfortable or like they're being put on the spot. Remember the aim is to make people feel at ease in your presence and to make them feel good, so as a general rule, ask questions about the topic at hand or ask them for advice on things you know they know about.

One of the most important reasons for asking questions is to get people talking. You want them to feel like you are interested in what they have to say, this way the conversation will flow more smoothly. Try not to ask too many yes or no questions as these give you very little time to think in between questions and may lead to awkward silences. Furthermore, yes and no questions can make people feel like they have to justify their answer with a longer response and that might make them feel under pressure. The best questions you can ask are actually the simplest ones.

When someone is telling you a story about something, ask them things like, "what was that like for you?", "what happened next?", "how did you resolve that issue?", "how did that feel?". Then *listen* to the answers and respond genuinely. As you do so, try to match their energy.

Say something like, "wow, I can't believe you got through that. I would've found that really hard!" or "That sounds incredible. I would've loved to have been there!".

If it feels like they have more to say, ask them to tell you more. Remember to make eye contact and lean in to show that you're interested. People love to talk about their experiences so as conversations like this progress, the chances are they will be feeling more and more comfortable in your presence. Conversations like this are also a great way to make someone feel like they have something interesting to say.

Try not to be fake or false in situations like this. Allow yourself to be natural while offering a forum for them to expand on their stories. This way they are much more likely to enjoy asking you about yours.

8. Be your true self
We've all heard the phrase "be yourself" countless times throughout our lives but what does that really mean? Technically we're *always* being ourselves; how could we possible be someone else? The idea of being our true selves is actually quite complicated. Inside we can always be our true selves but sometimes we do have to conform a little bit. If your true self is an opera singer, you can't very well walk into a silent meditation singing as loud as you can and then blame your behavior on being your true self!

However, there is something to be said for having your own thoughts, opinions, and beliefs. Conversations can get pretty boring if you're constantly trying to fit in or agree with everything everyone says. I'm not saying that you should be confrontational or that you should seek conflict, but it's important to know that you are interesting in your own way and that you're proud of that. You have had experiences that were entirely your own. You should be able to share your feelings and explore your thoughts with other people. Beware of any tendencies you might have of going along with what other people are saying even if you don't really agree with them. It is okay to disagree and to have well-rounded discussions with people.

If all you do is act the way other people do, your personality could get lost rather than shining through.

Be proud of what you know and be fearless in the face of that which you don't. Be proud of your beliefs and your accomplishments. If you are in the company of someone who cannot value who you are, they might not be the type of person you need to waste your time on.

9. Striking up a conversation
Starting conversations can be the hardest part of talking to people. There's usually a certain amount awkwardness and verbal fumbling around before you find your stride - especially if it's your first time talking to a particular person - but as with most things, you have to start somewhere. When it comes to getting people talking compliments and questions are always good starting points. Compliments will help ease tension while asking questions and seeking opinions both require answers.

For instance, if you're meeting someone for coffee and they come in carrying an interesting bag, express your interest by telling them that you like and ask them where they got it. If you're in a restaurant that's new to you, ask them if they've been there before and what they'd recommend on the menu. These are good icebreakers because they're not the most serious topics and they will help get the conversation flowing right off the bat. Next, think about anything unique that you know about the person and ask them questions about that.

For instance, if you know they work in the film industry, ask them something you've always wanted to know or simply ask them what that type of work is like. If you know they have children, ask how the kids are doing and what they're into. Remember that people like talking about themselves and questions like these aren't too imposing. Don't bother trying to make classic small talk. Asking someone if they "come here often" is a tired excuse for a conversation starter and unless there's been a recent hurricane, earthquake, or tsunami, the weather is just weather. So don't start out by talking about things that are likely to make someone yawn! Also, steer clear of questions that are too serious or could make someone uncomfortable. That means holding back on things like politics and other touchy subjects. Most importantly, relax and smile. It's important to remember that everyone will be a little bit nervous when talking to someone for the first time (or the first few times!). Try to talk slowly and remember to breathe.

Remember that conversations should be enjoyable so try not to put too much pressure on yourself and allow yourself to just have fun. If things get off to an awkward or clunky start, laugh it off and move on. There's no use holding on to embarrassing moments or letting your nerves get the better of you.

10. Try some verbal mirroring
Earlier you learned about mirroring with body language, but you can also mirror people with words. I'm obviously not recommending that you repeat everything someone else says or that you get involved in some strange sort of call and response exercise. Rather, I'm suggesting that you take something your conversational partner has said during the conversation and periodically reflect those things back to them, inviting them to clarify or elaborate on them.

For example, you might say something to the effect of, "You mentioned that you were ice skating over the weekend, is that something you've always done or something you're just trying out?" or "Earlier you referred to yourself as a 'bookworm'. Do you have a favorite book? Maybe you could recommend something to me…" or "So you make your own wine? How long have you been doing that? And how exactly do you go about that?"

This type of mirroring is reiterating the importance of what someone said. It's a way to show that you were listening and that you're interested in what they've been telling you. Doing this can also take some pressure off you if you feel like you've been doing most of the talking. These types of questions can also be helpful to clarify any misconceptions you may have had or anything you may have misheard.

11. Be complimentary

As Abraham Lincoln once said, 'everyone likes a compliment'. But the *type* of compliment you give is more important than you might think. Complimenting someone for the sake of complimenting them rarely comes off as sincere. We all like when people tell us we look nice, but we like it even more when they listen to our stories and compliment us on our real accomplishments in life.

As I said earlier, listening to someone is in itself a compliment as it makes the person feel good about what they're telling you. Beyond that though, there are so many more ways to truly compliment someone. Giving people descriptive appreciation for their accomplishments will always be a hit. Really try to tap into the things that make them feel important and compliment them on their hard work. Give credit where credit is due.

Resist the urge to just say, "good job". Instead, point out what they've accomplished and say something like, "I love what you've done with this. What made you think to do it that way? I wish I'd thought of that!" or "I love the colors you've chosen for your living room. Where did you get the inspiration for it?".

Compliments like these encourage people to talk about things they're proud of. They can bring an easy going and positive vibe to a conversation. Furthermore, compliments that are specific and descriptive will have far more impact than those that are generic or insincere. Pointing out the things someone is good at and praising them when they deserve it can be a great foundation for new relationships both in your personal life and your career.

12. Smile

There is a lot of research suggesting that how we look on the outside can change how we feel on the inside. A number of studies have shown that even something as simple as changing your clothes can change your behavior, your feelings of self worth, and your productivity. Smiling works in a similar way. The more we smile, the more happy and confident we actually feel. Smiling in social situations makes us appear and *feel* more relaxed and content. But in addition to that, smiling when you are talking to someone can relay a number of positive messages to them; thus affecting them positively. When we talk to people who are smiling we feel immediately more calm and secure in their presence.

Smiling is a way to show warmth, openness, friendliness, interest, and approval. It's also a great way to show that you are happy to be there and that you're on board with what someone is talking about. By literally changing your facial expression, both you and the person you're talking to are likely to feel better about the conversation. Just be careful not to smile when it's inappropriate to do so! In times of sadness, instead of allowing a full fledged grin to spread across your face, offer a small understanding smile and nod your head to show that you are listening and engaged.

13. Like people

It doesn't take a degree in psychology to know that people like to be liked. We need to feel a sense of likability from others. We need for people to be interested in us. Generally speaking, if you are in a conversation and you say a lot of negative things about other people, the person you're talking to is likely to feel a bit uneasy in your presence. After all, if you're gossipy and judgmental about other people behind their backs, what's to say you won't be the same way with this person? We can assume that people will develop a more positive opinion of you if you keep things on the positive.

So, if your conversation heads in the direction of talking about other people, try to talk mostly about people you like and talk about why you like them. This is especially important if you are talking about a mutual friend. Show that you care for other people and that you appreciate having people in your life by describing personality traits of theirs that you like. This type of positivity is a great foundation on which to build a conversation or a new relationship.

But the idea of liking people doesn't have to stop there. There are also ways you can show the person you're talking to that not only do you like other people, but you also like *them*. In order to show someone that you like them, encourage them to talk about things that matter to them. Ask meaningful questions about their children, their parents, their hobbies and achievements, anything you know to be important to them. Most importantly, don't be afraid to actually tell someone that you like specific things about them.

Telling someone that you respect the way they handled a situation or that you appreciate something they said can make both of you feel good. Conversations like these will make people remember you in a positive light. Smile at the world and it will smile back at you. Like people and they will like you back.

14. Do good research

When meeting up with someone, knowing a little bit about them can make a world of difference. It can help you break the ice at the start of the conversation and show your interest in them as the conversation progresses. There are a few simple ways you can achieve this. Firstly, if and where possible, try to prepare for meetings by learning about the other person's interests and passions. This doesn't mean you should stalk them (in person or online!) and it doesn't mean that you need to know everything about them.

After all, if you know everything about them already they'll either become suspicious of you or they'll simply have nothing more to tell you! Rather, if you have a mutual friend, ask them if they know anything that might help get the conversation started. Or if you've been emailing or texting the person in advance, ask them some questions about their hobbies and interests so that you'll have something to bring up in conversation later. Do your best to find out something about them that is unique or admirable so that you can comment on it when you're talking to them. Perhaps you're talking to a woman who has managed to climb the career ladder while being a single mother or maybe you're talking to someone who just got a promotion. Maybe you're talking to someone with a hidden talent or children who are high achievers.

Whatever it is, showing people that you admire them is a great way to make them happy to be in your presence. During your research, try to find something you have in common with them so that you'll have something you can fall back on if the conversation slows down a bit.

Do your children go to the same school?
Do you both like a certain restaurant?
Do you feel the same way about a particular sports team?

Whatever it is, having something in common means having more to talk about.

15. Be current
Keeping on top of current events can be lifesaver in social situations. Knowing what's going on in the world can connect you to other people no matter how well acquainted you are with them. Think of current events as commonality you share with strangers across the globe. You don't have to be knowledgeable about every single thing going on in the world but knowing a little bit about what's in the headlines can be a great way to start a conversation, not to mention making it possible for you to comment when other people bring these topics up. This is especially true in times of natural disasters or major political events. Having something to contribute or at least knowing what people are talking about will help you relate to them.

Remember that being current can also include knowing what's going on in music, sports, popular TV shows, arts and literature, podcasts, the list is endless. Just make sure that whatever the subject is, if you don't know much about it, don't fake it! If someone is talking about something you don't know much about, asking questions will show that you're interested even if you haven't had the chance to find these things out for yourself. Remember, you don't have to be an expert or have an opinion on everything. Simply being interested and asking others for their opinions will usually suffice.

Dealing With Specific Circumstances

Throughout our lives, we will all face a multitude of social situations that we find daunting, intimidating, and nerve-wracking. Some of us will struggle with things like public speaking and job interviews; others might worry more about things like dating and dealing with conflict. Though there is no way for us to avoid all such circumstances, there are ways that we can prepare ourselves for them and make them a bit easier to endure.

Dating and making new friends is possibly the most common concern when it comes to socializing in adulthood. Throughout our childhood and adolescence making friends was a far more natural process. Not only are our young lives centered around finding out who we are in relation to other people, but these years also present an abundance opportunities for us to socialize and experiment with social hierarchies and intimate relationships. As we age, these opportunities become fewer and fewer. Making and maintaining friendships becomes increasingly difficult as our careers and home lives take center stage. In fact, the number of friends we have usually drops dramatically once we've reached our late twenties. And when it comes to dating in adulthood, well, it can be a minefield.

Statistics have shown that these days, roughly half of the adults in American are single. This is a dramatic increase from the statistics taken just a few decades ago. Yet, even with this major shift, dating seems to be getting more and more difficult. There could be a number of factors contributing to this, from the global rise in text and email usage to the often unspoken decrease of social confidence. Although it is safe to say that dating can feel daunting and intimidating for anyone, for those of us who struggle with conversational confidence, the idea of going out on dates can leave you crippled with anxiety.

It may be helpful to think about making friends and dating as one and the same. When we first start dating someone, it can be hard not to think of every possible potential outcome. We might imagine ourselves living with this person twenty years from now or we might fast forward our thoughts all the way to a devastating break up.

However, being preoccupied with the future outcome of a new relationship can take a lot of enjoyment out of the getting to know you process. It can be hard to stop the mind from daydreaming in this way, but if you're living in 'what ifs', you might end up lacking the confidence and bravery it takes to actually get through and enjoy the early stages. This is why approaching dating the same way you would approach making a new friend, can dramatically lessen your anxiety and while increasing your potential for present and future happiness.

For those of us who have a tendency to rush through the beginning stages of relationships by either moving too fast or ending things before they even get started, it would be wise to explore why this is. Most often, both of these types of behaviors are rooted in some sort of fear. You may be scared that the relationship won't last or you might be equally scared that it will go quite well. There are a variety of reasons these fears and behaviors might occur. Having had difficult or unsuccessful relationships in the past, having limited experience with relationships, and having had troublesome childhoods are just a few. Problems like this can take some time to work through, but learning to understand your instincts and behavior when meeting new people might just be the key to your eventual happiness.

If dating is a difficulty in your life, start thinking about what might be making it so hard. Think about some of your past relationships (both intimate relationships and friendships) and try to identify any destructive patterns you might have.

Do you tend to dive into things head first?
Do you give too much of yourself?
Are you too guarded?
Do you only seek partners and/or friends whom you have to chase for their approval?
Do you have a tendency to push people away?

Do you become frightened if someone offers you too much attention?
Do you become devastated when they don't give you enough attention? Why?

Taking the time to reflect like this could help shed some light on your relationship patterns and help you figure out why they are the way they are. Gaining this type of knowledge means that you will be able to learn from your patterns and challenge them in future relationships.

As I said a moment ago, although making new friends can be daunting and uncomfortable at times, dating can be absolutely terrifying. This is why I suggest thinking about dating as simply making a new friend. Firstly, it takes the sting out of situation. Going on dates can put you under a lot of pressure, whereas thinking of them as simply meeting up with a friend can help ease your anxiety. In addition, the strongest intimate relationships are those that have grown out of great friendships. Friendships involve trust, lightness, mutuality, and respect; all of which have the potential to create a healthy foundation for an intimate relationship.

So, how exactly do we go about making new friends and lovers? Start by showing up on time! This simple act shows that you are reliable and that you really want to be there! Next, put all of your new skills on the table. Remember the person's name, mention things about them that you admire, listen intently, give genuine compliments, and most importantly, build on commonalities.

Whatever it is that you have in common with someone, think of that as your ticket in. Smile, relax, and remind yourself that the person you're meeting is probably just as nervous as you are.

Remember, don't touch someone unless you are 100% sure that you've been invited to, and always be polite! Finally, make sure to have some fun! Your enjoyment is just as important as anyone else's. Try not to let your anxiety steal the event from you.

Another situation where you might find conversation challenging is when you're talking to people who intimidate you. This might be your father-in-law, a particularly judgmental friend or relative, or someone you used to go out with. It might be someone who has a tendency to be condescending or overly critical of you. Or it may be someone who you think of as extremely successful or good looking. In situations like this, it's important to tell yourself right from the start that feeling intimidated by certain people is entirely normal, but thinking of yourself as inferior, could be damaging to your self confidence and make social situations more awkward than they need to be.

Often meetings like this get blown out of proportion. We might worry about an upcoming event for weeks, getting ourselves wound up way more than necessary. If you're prone to 'stewing' about an upcoming event like this, challenge yourself to do something productive with that habit. Rather than worrying, think about some ways you might be able to make the conversation more enjoyable.

Think about the things you have in common with this person and how you might use them to ease the tension between you or get them on your side. Visualize yourself having successful a conversation with that person. Think about how you want the conversation to go and how you'd like to be perceived. Ask yourself: Is there any *real* reason things couldn't go the way you want them to?

Is there any reason you actually should be intimidated by this person or is this feeling rooted in something else?
Is it possible that the people you talk to might also be nervous or intimidated by you?
Most importantly, what happens if it doesn't go well?
Have you had things go badly before? Did you survive?

When you are talking to this person, remember not to fidget or look around a lot. Sit or stand with your chin up and chest raised. Don't cross your arms, touch your face and neck, or hold things in front of your chest. Even if you are feeling extremely intimidated, keeping your body language in check is a great way to hide your anxiety.

Try to think about yourself and other people as equals no matter what differences lie between you. You are both human beings. You both face challenges and difficulties in life. You are both good at something. If someone is rude or hurtful toward you, let it roll off of you like water off a duck's back. Be polite no matter what. Try not to let people to have so much power over you that they can alter the way you feel about yourself or how you behave. Most importantly, make a resolve to live up to your own personal values. No matter what happens in a conversation like this, be proud of who you are and stay true to yourself. At the end of the day, no matter how the conversation goes, you should be able to walk away with your head held high.

When it comes to being intimidated, few things are as nerve wracking as making speeches and attending job interviews. If you think about it, both of these acts involve a certain amount of *selling yourself*. But if you struggle with low self-esteem or conversational anxiety, it's hardly surprising to think about just how emotionally activating these situations can be. Having an audience - regardless of how big or how small - can be petrifying. Feeling like you're being judged on every word you utter is just downright unpleasant, no matter what the circumstance. For situations like these, few things can help as much as punctuality, preparedness, and perspective.

So, once again, start by being on time! Punctuality makes you look like you care. Being late is disrespectful and unprofessional. If you're attending a job interview and there is some reason why you are going to be late, call ahead to explain the situation and express your apologies rather than just turning up late and fumbling through an excuse as you introduce yourself.

Next, show that you are prepared. For job interviews make sure to take the time to research the company before you get there. Learn about their values and their mission. Think about how you might fit into a company like that and how your skills and knowledge might help their cause. Try not to rehearse lines about yourself as this can come across as odd and a bit too self-serving. Rather, make sure you listen to the questions you're asked and answer them to the best of your ability. If you're unsure of what an interviewer is asking you at any point, ask for them to clarify rather than trying to fake your way through it.

During the interview, mention the things you know about the company and ask a few questions about how they've achieved the things they have. Just like when you're speaking to an individual, showing interest in a company is complimentary. It will show that not only do you have the skills for the job, but that you will take an active interest in it.

As for speeches, preparedness is fundamental. In this case, whether you're doing a speech at a wedding or a small presentation at work, practice makes perfect. Write your speech as early as possible so that you will have plenty of time to get it right. Practice reading your speech out loud. Doing this may feel strange but it will be much more beneficial than reciting it in your head. Practicing your speech aloud in front of a mirror or rehearsing it with a small group of friends will help you get the pace right and iron out any parts that don't flow well. Also, the more you practice your speech, the more comfortable you'll be when the time comes.

No matter what the situation, maintain perspective. Often, the reason we get so nervous before making a speech or attending a job interview is because we've made it way more important in our head than it really is. Though making a mistake in front of a group of people never feels good, having the ability to laugh at it and shake it off is really important for your self esteem. Everyone makes mistakes, everyone says something stupid from time to time, but if we live our lives focusing on our mistakes, how will we ever get to enjoy life? Before getting on stage or being called in for your interview, ask yourself what's the worst thing that can happen?

You might trip and fall or you might not get the job.
You might feel embarrassed or disappointed. So what?
Have you felt embarrassed and disappointed before? Did you survive? Did those feelings eventually cease to be so important?

Chances are, whatever you're afraid of, it has happened before and it will happen again. These are merely the experiences we all have in life. They do not have the power to make or break you. Keeping perspective will help you stay calm and relaxed.

Finally, having to face and cope with conflict can be one of the hardest parts of life. Whether we have a disagreement with our colleagues, we have to resolve a personal or business administrative issue, or a relationship turns sour, conflict is rarely easy to overcome. Very few people welcome conflict and confrontation but many times, it's simply unavoidable. Misunderstandings happen, people have widely varying opinions. We all have different perspectives based on our individual experiences and beliefs. But these differences do not have to lead to uncomfortable social awkwardness and they do not have to divide us.

Conflict doesn't have to be all that bad. If you think about it, the moments we deal with conflict can be character building. We can learn from all of our experiences, good and bad. But conflict also presents a situation where being *relatable* can have its greatest influence. First of all, people don't enjoy being barked at or being treated like they are inferior. And as we know, human beings rarely respond well to know-it-alls and people that are unnecessarily pushy with their personal beliefs. Unfortunately, we can't change other people. We can however, change the way we behave in their presence - we can be relatable - and that might just influence them to change some of their own behaviors.

In many circumstances, treating people with respect and showing that you value their opinion will be enough to bring conflict to a halt. You can do this by saying something like, "I respect where you're coming from" or "I understand", or by simply listening to their side of things. If you can find a solution to the disagreement by being relatable, you may be able to turn a negative situation into a positive one. By that I mean admitting any of your own faults or flaws in the matter. Admitting anything you may have done wrong, judged poorly, or misunderstood is often enough to encourage others to do the same.

Remember, making mistakes and being flawed is not a weakness, it's just human nature. If you can find no fault in the situation at hand, try to think of a time in your life when you felt the way your conversational partner is feeling. If it feels appropriate, see if relaying that story might be a way out of your current conflict. Letting people know that you've been 'in their shoes' before can make them behave in a less antagonistic or defensive way. Just be careful not to sound condescending or patronizing if you do this. Try to be humble and empathetic.

Sometimes, no matter how much you try to resolve it, conflict just goes on and on. What then? First of all, it's important to recognize when a conversation has reached a stalemate and there's nothing more you can say or do to change the situation. You have to know when to call it quits. If someone is being unreasonable or rude, sometimes the best thing you can do is agree to disagree and walk away. Other times, you might want to suggest changing the subject so as to try to rescue some amount of good humor in the conversation.

If someone has been drinking or they are being unnecessarily confrontational, the problem might be theirs and theirs alone. It is absolutely fine to be assertive about how you're feeling and leave. Just try not to get swept away in the mood. Don't scream and shout. Don't accuse or scold anyone. Keeping your cool in conflict is something people will remember. Losing your cool in conflict is something they'll remember more.

Progress With Life, Do Not Let The Fear Hold You Back

Being a great conversationalist isn't about being the coolest or smartest person in town. It doesn't mean knowing the answer to everything or being the most accomplished or successful person on earth. As you have progressed through this book, you have learned that there is far more to conversation than people may realize. Being the type of person that people want to talk to means being relatable and sincere. It is something that anyone can learn to do. Social anxiety and conversational nervousness are extremely common in today's world. They are difficulties that are often made worse by avoiding social situations, but they can be made dramatically easier with a little bit of practice and determination.

As a good conversationalist, your role is to make people feel at ease in your company. Smiling and showing a genuine interest in others can be immensely more powerful than being an expert in your field. People seek feelings of approval and importance throughout their lives. Conversation is one of the most important methods of achieving these fundamental social needs. By asking people meaningful questions, listening intently as they speak, and offering them sincere compliments, you can become the type of person that people want to be around.

Most importantly, by maintaining perspective, lightening up, being positive and having fun with people, your experience with conversations will no longer be stressful and anxiety provoking. Rather, they'll be easy, productive, and enjoyable!

I wish you all the best with your future journey through life.

facebook.com/drjenniferalison

[Subscribe](#) to the Dr. Jennifer Alison mailing list for news of new releases, free eBooks and exclusive extra content.

[Sign up by clicking here.](#)

Printed in Poland
by Amazon Fulfillment
Poland Sp. z o.o., Wrocław